STUDIES IN THE TEXT OF THE NEW TESTAMENT

A. T. ROBERTSON, M.A., D.D., LL.D., LITT.D.

Books by Professor A. T. ROBERTSON, D.D.

THE ENGLISH NEW TESTAMENT AS A WHOLE:
Syllabus for New Testament Study.
The Student's Chronological New Testament.
Studies in the New Testament.
New Testament History.

THE GREEK NEW TESTAMENT:
A Short Grammar of the Greek New Testament.
A Grammar of the Greek New Testament in the Light of Historical Research.
The Minister and His Greek New Testament.
An Introduction to the Textual Criticism of the New Testament.
Studies in the Text of the New Testament.

THE GOSPELS AND JESUS:
A Harmony of the Gospels for Students of the Life of Christ.
A Commentary on Matthew.
Studies in Mark's Gospel.
Luke the Historian in the Light of Research.
A Translation of Luke's Gospel.
The Divinity of Christ in the Gospel of John.
John the Loyal.
The Pharisees and Jesus.
Epochs in the Life of Jesus.
Keywords in the Teaching of Jesus.
The Teaching of Jesus Concerning God the Father.
The Christ of the Logia.
The Mother of Jesus: Her Problems and Her Glory.

PAUL:
Epochs in the Life of Paul.
Paul the Interpreter of Christ.
Paul's Joy in Christ.
The Glory of the Ministry.
The New Citizenship.

OTHER STUDIES IN THE NEW TESTAMENT:
Studies in the Epistle of James.
Making Good in the Ministry: A Sketch of John Mark.
Types of Preachers in the New Testament.

BIOGRAPHY:
Life and Letters of John A. Broadus.

STUDIES IN THE TEXT OF THE NEW TESTAMENT

BY

A. T. ROBERTSON, M.A., D.D., LL.D., LITT.D.

CHAIR OF NEW TESTAMENT INTERPRETATION,
SOUTHERN BAPTIST THEOLOGICAL SEMINARY,
LOUISVILLE, KY.

Πρόσεχε τῇ ἀναγνώσει

WIPF & STOCK · Eugene, Oregon

Wipf and Stock Publishers
199 W 8th Ave, Suite 3
Eugene, OR 97401

Studies in the Text of the New Testament
By Robertson, A. T.
ISBN 13: 978-1-5326-0363-1
Publication date 7/30/2016
Previously published by Doran Books, 1926

TO

REV. E. Y. MULLINS, D.D., LL.D.

PRESIDENT OF THE SOUTHERN BAPTIST THEOLOGICAL SEMINARY
AND PROFESSOR OF THEOLOGY, 1899–
PRESIDENT OF THE SOUTHERN BAPTIST CONVENTION, 1921–23
PRESIDENT OF THE BAPTIST WORLD ALLIANCE, 1923–

*In grateful appreciation of his sympathetic
interest in my studies and work*

ACKNOWLEDGMENTS

Thanks are hereby extended to the following journals for permission to use such of the chapters as appeared in their pages: *The Expositor* (London), *The Expository Times* (Edinburgh), *The Homiletic Review* (New York), *The Biblical Review* (New York), *The Methodist Review* (Nashville), *The Expositor* (Cleveland), *The Sunday School Times* (Philadelphia), *The Record of Christian Work* (East Northfield).

PREFACE

My interest in the Greek New Testament grows with each year and includes the problems of text as well as those of grammar. The history of the effort to restore the original text of the Greek New Testament is outlined in my *Introduction to the Textual Criticism of the New Testament* (1925). But there are numerous sidelights that justify a fuller discussion of various points. Some of these appear in the present volume. The general reader will be glad to see several sides of a technical subject. An enormous amount of hard work has been done through the centuries by painstaking scholars in order to preserve and restore the text, like the recent remarkable work of Dr. B. H. Streeter in *The Four Gospels* (1925). There is an element of romance and of pathos in it all that calls for appreciation and gratitude. We are the heirs of a noble past. Slowly new light is turned on difficult problems. Each discovery comes at the cost of toil and sacrifice. But it is all worth while if so be that we can get the mind and the words of Christ.

A. T. ROBERTSON.

CONTENTS

CHAPTER		PAGE
I	THE AUTOGRAPHS OF THE NEW TESTAMENT	15
II	ROMANCE AND TRAGEDY IN THE HISTORY OF THE NEW TESTAMENT TEXT	27
III	HOW THE TEXTUS RECEPTUS WON ITS PLACE	43
IV	WHY TEXTUAL CRITICISM FOR THE PREACHER	54
V	LOSSES AND GAINS IN THE CRITICAL TEXT OF THE NEW TESTAMENT	65
VI	STREETER'S THEORY OF LOCAL TEXTS	76
VII	WHEN THE WESTERN TEXT IS RIGHT	80
VIII	SOME INTERESTING READINGS IN THE WASHINGTON CODEX OF THE GOSPELS	94
IX	PAUL AND HIS BOOKS	102
X	EARLY ENGLISH BIBLES	113
XI	THE REVISED NEW TESTAMENT AFTER FORTY YEARS	128
XII	RECENT TRANSLATIONS OF THE NEW TESTAMENT	137
XIII	WRONG CHAPTER AND VERSE DIVISIONS IN THE NEW TESTAMENT	149
XIV	THE TEXT OF MATTHEW 1:16	162
XV	THE TEXT OF JOHN 1:13	174
XVI	THE IMPLICATIONS IN LUKE'S PREFACE	186

STUDIES IN THE TEXT
OF THE NEW TESTAMENT

STUDIES IN THE TEXT OF THE NEW TESTAMENT

CHAPTER I

THE AUTOGRAPHS OF THE NEW TESTAMENT

There are few things in history more fascinating to scholars than the story of the preservation of the text of the Greek New Testament from the first century A.D. till now. The whole thing is a marvel of God's goodness and grace. Conflicting attitudes mark the centuries as men were indifferent, hostile, reverential, even idolatrous, in their treatment of the books of the New Testament.

In the New Testament itself one sees diversity. Paul is concerned that his First Epistle to the Thessalonians be read in public, or at least made public: "I adjure you by the Lord that this epistle be read unto all the brethren" (1 Thess. 5:27). It is a solemn appeal, "I put you under oath." He expected to be obeyed in "this epistle" (2 Thess. 3:14). He appeals to his signature in each Epistle to prove its genuineness (2 Thess. 3:17). See also Colossians 4:18: "The salutation of me Paul with mine own hand." He warns the Thessalonians against spurious epistles under his name (2 Thess. 2:2).

It seems strange to us that Paul felt it necessary to make this warning when writing the earliest of his Epistles that have been preserved to us. But Paul had been grievously misunderstood at Thessalonica in what he had said about the Second Coming of Christ (1 Thess. 5: 1; 2 Thess. 2: 1; 3: 10). And it was common enough at that time for men to write in the name of another man of distinction who was dead. These writings were called pseudonymous, under a false name. Paul evidently does not relish the idea that any one should sign his name to a letter to advance his own ideas and interests. Precisely this issue is raised today about 2 Peter, for in 1: 1 the writer claims to be Simon Peter. No such issue is raised about Hebrews, for the author says nothing about his own name.

Paul wrote some epistles that we do not now possess. In 1 Corinthians 5: 9, "I wrote unto you in my epistle," he refers to an epistle that has been lost. We probably have the same thing in 2 Corinthians 2: 4, "For out of much affliction and anguish of heart I wrote unto you with many tears." This seems to be an epistle that came in between our 1 Corinthians and 2 Corinthians. The writing of this epistle made Paul sorry at first and made the Corinthians still more sorry (2 Cor. 7: 8), but it did the work and brought the majority of the church round to Paul's side in the controversy there.

Paul expected some of his Epistles to be passed on from church to church, for he urges the Colossians to send this Epistle on to the church in Laodicea after it had been read by them (Col. 4: 16) and to get also the Epistle from Laodicea that he had sent to them (our

Ephesians). It is not clear whether the autograph copy was sent on in each case or a copy made. Probably a copy was made, for the oldest manuscripts, Codex Sinaiticus and Codex Vaticanus, have no name in Ephesians 1:1. The Apocalypse includes a special letter to each of seven churches in the Province of Asia, and there the text of the Apocalypse must either be copied or passed on from church to church after a public reading to each church (Rev. 1:3, "he that readeth, and they that hear the words of the prophecy"). Manuscripts were costly to copy. The material itself was an item of expense. An epistle addressed to a church would be read in open meeting by a competent reader while the audience listened to the reading. This is the picture that we have presented to us in Revelation 1:3.

It is not hard to picture the interest and even excitement in Corinth when another letter came from Paul. The church was keenly divided about Paul and Apollos and Cephas. There was even a Christ party. The Judaizers had come out and had fanned the flame of faction that arose over the respective merits of Apollos and Paul. Paul wrote sharply and keenly rebuked the spirit of dissension and the gross sins that were manifest in this church. Some, the majority, were made sorry unto repentance and came over to loyalty to Paul (2 Cor. 1:14; 2:5; 7:9). But there was a stubborn minority who scouted both Paul and his Epistles. Their scorn stung Paul to defend both his letters and his life, "that I may not seem as if I would terrify you by my letters. For, His letters, they say, are weighty and strong; but his bodily presence is weak, and his speech of no account" (2 Cor. 10: 9–10). Paul's enemies in Corinth, the Judaizers, had to admit the pith and point of his Epistles. Today they rank as the greatest letters in all history. The church in Corinth had them in black and white. They counted heavily for the Pauline gospel of grace in Corinth. The church there did allow two of the four Corinthian Epistles to perish, but we can thank God for the preservation of the two that we do have.

The Judaizers found it difficult to make light of Paul's letters, so they took to making fun of his personal appearance. They admitted that he was a great letter writer, but charged him with having an insignificant personality and with inconsistency in his conduct. He was always talking about coming to Corinth, but he was evidently afraid to come. As a matter of fact, Paul had changed his plans about going over directly from Ephesus to Corinth and had postponed his visit there to give them a chance to change their conduct. "But I call God to witness upon my soul, that to spare you I forbare to come unto Corinth" (2 Cor. 1: 23). It is probable that Paul did not have as commanding an appearance as some men, perhaps one not equal to that of Apollos or of Peter. There is a tradition that he was a hunchback. For myself, I do not believe it. But there is no way to disprove it. The so-called pictures of Peter and Paul cannot be depended upon as genuine. The Galatians had been more considerate and had not rejected or despised Paul because of a trial in his flesh, however repugnant it may have been to them (Gal. 4: 13–14). They had received him as courteously as if he had been an angel

THE AUTOGRAPHS OF THE NEW TESTAMENT 19

of God or Jesus Christ himself. This "infirmity of the flesh" may have been eye trouble or almost anything. But here in Corinth Paul's enemies brutally attacked his personal appearance in order to discount his power and his prestige. But his Epistles they could not discredit.

What a priceless treasure it would be if one could find the autograph copy of one of Paul's Epistles. But, even if we should have that good fortune, we should probably not have Paul's own handwriting, but only his signature at the close (2 Thess. 3:17), save in the short letter to Philemon which was apparently written in Paul's own hand: "I Paul write it with mine own hand, I will repay it" (Philem. 17). This sentence was a collectible note of hand on Paul and indicates that in this instance Paul did not dictate his letter to an amanuensis as was his usual custom. In the Epistle to the Romans we even know the name of the scribe who wrote out the letter for Paul: "I Tertius, who write the epistle, salute you in the Lord" (Rom. 16:22). This is probably what Peter means about Silvanus (Silas) who may also have been the bearer of his Epistle to the five provinces of Asia Minor (1 Peter 1:1): "By Silvanus, our faithful brother, as I account him, I have written unto you briefly" (1 Pet. 5:12).

It is not certain what Paul means in Galatians 6:11, "See with how large letters I write unto you with mine own hand." We do know that here he is writing with his own hand, whether he had written all the Epistle up to this point or not. From now to the close he uses the pen himself. The Authorized Version had it thus: "Ye see how large a letter I have written unto you with mine own hand." This was a mere mistranslation, because the Greek word is plural, not singular. Paul is not calling attention to the size of the Epistle, but to the size of the letters which he uses in writing.

Chrysostom suggests that Paul did not know how to write well and made his letters with difficulty and of large size like a child learning how to write. But he became so earnest at this point that he took the pen himself and printed the rest of the Epistle in big (capital) letters. Theodore of Mopsuestia thinks that Paul here uses large letters because he himself neither blushes at nor denies the things that were being said. Theodoret considers that Paul means, not with what large letters, but with what poor letters, he has written to the Galatians. Jerome thinks that Paul knew Hebrew better than Greek, and yet because of his love for the Galatians he attempted what he was not able to do and so had to make large Greek letters. Sir W. M. Ramsay suggests that Paul made a sort of placard or advertisement of these closing verses of the Epistle. He had said in 3:1 that Jesus Christ was openly set forth (*proegraphe*) crucified before them. That figure of a placard may be the idea here. On the other hand Paul may simply be calling attention to the large capital letters that he is here employing instead of the usual running or cursive hand of letter writing. He is writing with the book or literary hand rather than with the running hand of the average amanuensis.

One other theory is advanced which is, that Paul had poor eyesight and could only write with large letters. Whatever the fact may be, it remains that Paul does call attention to the size of the letters as proof of his

THE AUTOGRAPHS OF THE NEW TESTAMENT 21

earnestness in what he is saying. But one can hardly say that Paul did not know Greek well enough to write it with ease. On the contrary he shows a real mastery of the Greek of the time, the *koine*, and in his Epistles he has passages of great power and beauty as, for instance, Romans 8, and 1 Corinthians 13 and 15. Paul knew his Greek as well as his Hebrew (Aramaic) and his Latin.

It is remarkable that Jesus wrote nothing, so far as we know, save once on the ground, and no one knows what He wrote then. But it is idle to say that Jesus did not know how to write. He spoke both Aramaic and Greek at will, and employed whichever language suited his audience best, as did Paul in Jerusalem (Acts 21: 37, 40). But Jesus wrote his words in human hearts and human lives. His blood on the cross carries his eternal message of love. We have the chirography of Christ on the Cross in his blood by which he rubbed out the handwriting (*to cheirographon*) of legal obligation against us (Col. 2: 14).

Some of the short letters, like 2 and 3 John or Philemon, could have been written on wax tablets, but not the longer ones. These were written either upon papyrus or parchment. The shorter books were very likely upon papyrus while the longer ones may have been written on parchment. Both were in use in the first century A.D., though papyrus was more common. By the end of the fourth century parchment or vellum had pretty well displaced papyrus for book purposes. The vellum suited much better and could be made into codices or leaf-books, like our modern printed books. The papyrus rolls were hard to handle and could not contain a book of any size except with great difficulty. We know that John used "paper and ink" for his second Epistle (12), as also he wrote his third "with ink and pen" (13). This would be on papyrus. But Paul was acquainted with parchment also, for he asked Timothy to bring "the books, especially the parchments" (2 Tim. 4:13). Here he draws a distinction between the ordinary papyrus rolls (*biblia*), such as the attendant in the synagogue handed to Jesus in Capernaum (Luke 4:17, 20), and the more precious parchments (*membranas*).

One wishes that he knew what were these books and parchments that were so dear to Paul. They were evidently rolls and codices that he had used much and that he prized highly. He had taken them with him on his travels in the East, but for some reason he had left them with his cloak at Troas with Carpus. The "cloak," in fact, may be a "book-wrap" as it often is. I hope that Carpus had taken good care of both the wrap and the books. I dislike to see books treated badly, especially if they are good books. Portions of the Old Testament in Hebrew or in Greek were probably in the list. It is even possible that the Gospel of Mark or the Gospel of Luke were among them. Paul had found Mark useful to him for ministering (2 Tim. 4:11), for Mark had made good again after his lapse at Perga (Acts 13:13). Mark had been with Paul in Rome, and Paul had commended him to the Colossians (Col. 4:10). But at any rate, we see here Paul's hunger for his old books. It is even possible, though unlikely, that copies of some of his own Epistles or some of his notes were in the pile of manuscripts left with Carpus.

It is probable that all the Gospels and the Acts were written on parchment and in the literary book hand of the period. Certainly Luke (see my *Luke the Historian in the Light of Research*) had the habits of a literary man (Luke 1: 1-4). He gathered his materials from books and from eyewitnesses (oral testimony), in addition to his own personal knowledge. He sifted the whole of the material and wrote an orderly and accurate account for the better instruction of Theophilus, to whom he dedicates both the Gospel and the Acts, and of all who read what he writes. Here we see a more conscious literary effort than in Paul's Epistles. Luke makes use of sources, and he uses them with great skill, though the earmarks crop out here and there. Luke, like Paul, was a man of literary culture, as well as of great genius. His Gospel was called by Renan the most beautiful book in all the world. The Acts is ranked by Ramsay as the work of the greatest historian in the world.

Ramsay calls Paul the greatest philosopher of all time. Dr. J. Rendel Harris is now arguing that Paul shows acquaintance with Pindar as well as with Euripides and Aristophanes. Be that as it may, his Epistles take first rank among all the letters of the world. It is not to be supposed that Paul had any such idea of his writings when he wrote them, though he felt the importance of his messages. He did not pose or attitudinize in his letters. He was after the verdict, and he got it. Deissmann (*Bible Studies*, and *Light from the Ancient East*) insists that Paul wrote letters, not epistles. Hebrews is an example of epistles of a formal nature, more like an essay or an oration than a private letter. Deissmann holds that Paul wrote no literary epistles, but only private letters. There is a point in the distinction he draws, but he pushes it too far. Romans is not a private letter, though chapter 16 is devoted to personal matters. Paul expected his letters to be read in public to various churches. They are direct messages to actual persons and churches, but they carry messages of eternal value for all today as for all of that time. Deissmann is right in his protest against Blass, who claims that Paul was a student of rhetoric and oratory and that his Epistles are full of conscious rhythm and rhetorical devices. There is rhythm at times in Paul's letters, but it is the unconscious sweep of a great soul aflame with passion, not the artificial rhetoric of the mere declaimer.

The Romans had no postal system save for state purposes. So Paul had to rely on the visits of friends to carry his Epistles, as when Phoebe went from Cenchrea to Rome (Rom. 16: 1) or Epaphroditus was sent back by Paul from Rome to Philippi (Phil. 2: 25). The messenger would be able to give additional information not in the letter, as Tychicus to Colossae (Col. 4: 7), and to Ephesus and Laodicea (Eph. 6: 21–22; Col. 4: 16).

The use of different amanuenses explains some of the variations in vocabulary and style between the several groups of Paul's Epistles. Jerome pointed out long ago that Peter probably employed different interpreters for his two Epistles, Silvanus for the First, an unknown one for the Second unless he wrote this without an interpreter. This fact does not explain everything, but it does have its bearing beyond a doubt. In the same way John in the Apocalypse may be writing alone while in the Gospel and Epistles he may have had others to read over his writings. Many medieval manuscripts of the Fourth Gospel picture John dictating his Gospel to a disciple named Prochorus (see Milligan's *New Testament Documents*, p. 23). A certain amount of liberty may have been left to the amanuensis. "In dictating, the Apostle would have clearly before his mind's eye the actual persons and circumstances of those to whom he was writing, and broken constructions and sudden changes of subject prove how often the eager rush of his words overmastered the grammatical and orderly sequence of his thought" (Milligan, *op. cit.*, p. 27).

There is little hope that we shall ever see an autograph copy of any book in the Greek New Testament. Casper René Gregory (*Canon and Text of the New Testament*, p. 512) felt that the last leaf of Mark's Gospel which was probably torn off may yet be found: "I regard it nevertheless as one of the possibilities of future finds that we receive this Gospel with its own authentic finish." But the brittle papyrus would not last outside of the dry sand of Egypt and the ashes of Herculaneum. It is certain that Christians began to write about Jesus very early, as Luke implies (1: 1-4). Sir W. M. Ramsay thinks that Matthew wrote down his *Logia*, the Q of Harnack, the *Logia* of Papias, the very year that Jesus died. The papyri of Egypt show us how widespread writing was in the first century A.D. There were shorthand writers in plenty. Business man as Matthew was, he could easily have taken down in Aramaic shorthand notes of discourses of Jesus.

The papyri letters with their salutations and signatures furnish us with precise parallels for Paul's Epistles. The very language of the New Testament appears in the papyri. We do not have the autographs of the New Testament books, but we can look at these papyrus rolls and easily imagine what they looked like. And we have over four thousand Greek manuscripts of portions of the New Testament. "The books of the New Testament as preserved in extant documents assuredly speak to us in every important respect in language identical with that in which they spoke to those for whom they were originally written" (Hort, *Introduction*, p. 284).

CHAPTER II

ROMANCE AND TRAGEDY IN THE HISTORY OF THE NEW TESTAMENT TEXT

There are few subjects with as little popular appeal as the textual criticism of the New Testament. One thinks of musty monasteries, or of the scholarly recluse remote from the life of men with all its struggles and aspirations. But, just as progress in knowledge of the wonders of the stars is linked with exact mathematical calculations and measurements, so the preservation of the N. T. text from the first century till now is marked by heroism and tragedy that challenge our interest and our gratitude. If the Bible is worth half to the world what its sharpest critics admit, it is certainly due a certain amount of consideration for the marvellous way in which it has come down to us.

The human interest starts with the beginning. One can feel Paul's indignation over the effort of some pious cranks in Thessalonica to palm off spurious epistles with his name as author, in order to bolster up their false interpretation of his preaching in Thessalonica (2 Thess. 2:1–3). He was compelled to call attention to his own signature at the close of each Epistle as the proof of its genuineness, just as bankers today watch the handwriting of the signature to a cheque (3:17). Criticism of the Pauline Epistles began with the beginning, and it has continued until now. In Corinth, Paul's adversaries admitted the power of his letters without trying to forge his name to any, but they ridiculed his personal presence (2 Cor. 10:9–11). Paul usually dictated his Epistles, and it is interesting to see Tertius, the amanuensis for the Epistle to the Romans, slyly slipping in his own greeting (Rom. 16:22). There is a pathetic interest in the "large letters" used by Paul in writing with his own hand in large uncials (like a child's print) the passionate close of the Epistle to the Galatians (6:11), if that fact is due to his poor eyes (4:15). But if he had an acute eye-trouble, so common in the glaring sun in the East, that trial or "temptation" (4:14) may have been temporary. Certainly Paul had his books, both papyrus and parchment, and used them, and missed them when without them (2 Tim. 4:13).

It was not easy to preserve books in the first century A.D. Most of them were written on the brittle papyrus of which we now have so many fragments from Egypt. There they have been preserved in the dry sands of the rubbish-heaps or wrapped round mummies in the tombs. But the N.T. autographs probably perished quickly, though fortunately not before copies were made of them. Paul meant his Epistles to be read in public (1 Thess. 5:27), and they were sometimes passed from church to church, as was true of those to Colossæ and Laodicea (our Ephesians), as he expressly directed should be done (Col. 4:16). Probably each church had a copy made before the Epistle was passed on to another church.

The more important, or more lengthy, books were

ROMANCE AND TRAGEDY

written on parchment, as was probably the case with St. Luke's Gospel and the Acts. At first, books were made on sheets of papyrus or parchment fastened together into a roll. But in the fourth century the codex had supplanted the roll, and parchment had taken the place of papyrus.

The early copies of various books of the N. T. were made separately, one book by itself. By degrees the Gospels were bound together, the Pauline Epistles together, and so on. It was only after the parchment codex came into use with its leaves like our modern books, that all the N. T. books could be bound into one volume, and finally the entire Greek Bible as in the Codex Sinaiticus (ℵ) and the Codex Vaticanus (B). But it was not merely carelessness in copying and indifference in the use of books, like losing the outside leaf, as is possible in St. Mark's Gospel, that the N. T. had to suffer. It is amazing how some people today misuse books. One of the worst incidents in the repeated persecutions that the early Christians had to undergo was the wholesale destruction of the N. T. books by imperial command, and by the rage of the pagans. It was like the case of Antiochus Epiphanes in Jerusalem, when he tore down the altar of Jehovah and set up an altar to Jupiter (Zeus), with destruction of all copies of the sacred books of the Jews. Dr. Hort puts the situation with his usual sobriety of statement when he says: "Destruction of books, which had played so considerable a part in textual history at the threshold of the Constantinian Age, was repeated again and again on a larger scale, with the important difference that now no reaction followed. The ravages of the barbarians and Mahomet annihilated the MSS of vast regions, and narrowly limited the area within which transcription was carried on. Thus an immense number of the MSS representing texts farthest removed in locality from Antiochian (or Constantinopolitan) influence perished entirely, leaving no successors to contribute readings to other living texts or to transmit their own texts to the present day" (*Introduction*, pp. 142 f., vol. ii. of *The New Testament in the Original Greek*, 1882). One must let his imagination fill out this picture. One would go to the stake with a precious copy of Paul's Epistles or of the Gospel of St. John. A whole family, house and all, would be burned up by the ruthless Goths and Vandals. The wonder is that anything remained. Constantine about A.D. 331 ordered fifty manuscript copies of the Greek Bible prepared for the churches of Constantinople by Eusebius of Cæsarea. Caspar René Gregory thought that B and א were two of these fifty. That is quite possible, though there is no evidence that either of these manuscripts was ever in Constantinople. But it is certain that the hatred against Christianity and Christians included the books of the N. T. For a while it did look as if these priceless books might perish from the face of the earth. What the result would have been to the world one can contemplate with horror.

We may be grateful for the early translations of the Greek N. T., for they helped to circulate the book in the language of the people and to preserve it for us today. It would make a fascinating story in itself to tell how the Diatessaron of Tatian has been rediscovered from two Arabic manuscripts of the eleventh century. The Diatessaron or Harmony of the Four Gospels in connected narrative was long lost, but it is now accessible in several good English translations. It is not known whether it was made first in Greek or in Syriac, but it played a large part in the history of the N. T. in Syriac. Von Soden holds that this Diatessaron of Tatian, dating from the second half of the second century, was the main disturbing factor in the text of the N. T., as Origen's Hexapla was in the text of the O. T. Dr. J. Rendel Harris thinks that Tatian's Encratism appears in his reading that John the Baptist ate "milk and honey." The recovery of two manuscripts of the Old Syriac has thrown new light on the Syriac versions and made it plain that the Peshitta version was not early, but late. It was Dr. W. Cureton, of the British Museum, who in 1848 edited the Syriac version of the Gospels now known as the Curetonian Syriac. In 1892 Mrs. Lewis and Mrs. Gibson, the distinguished twin-sisters of Cambridge, found another Syriac Gospel manuscript in the Convent of St. Catherine on Mount Sinai. It is a palimpsest and is another Old Syriac document of great value. These discoveries whet one's appetite for more research.

New manuscripts of the Egyptian Versions are throwing fresh light on the various Coptic versions, of which three are known (the Sahidic, the Bashmuric, the Bohairic). Only recently Sir W. M. Flinders-Petrie has told of the discovery of a Coptic manuscript of the Gospel of St. John older than any now known, and of a different dialect also. The oldest Latin translation was made in North Africa, where Greek was little understood, and, later, one was made in Europe. It was in A.D. 405 that Jerome finished his thorough revision of the previous translations. Jerome made the translation at the request of Pope Damasus, but all the same he knew and wrote in advance that the people would not like it. He had some better Greek manuscripts than lay behind the Old Latin versions, but he lost his temper at the abuse heaped upon him by those who preferred the Old Latin to which they had become accustomed. "Dean Burgon's opposition to the English revision of 1881 seemed to us serious, but it was mere child's play beside the antagonism shown in the fourth century" (Gregory, *Canon and Text of the New Testament*, p. 411). It was literally centuries before Jerome's work came into general use, not before the ninth century, and the Anglo-Saxons copied the Old Latin instead of the Vulgate. The name "Vulgate" does not seem to have been attached to the work of Jerome till the Council of Trent, April 8, 1546, and then only as an adjective in the sense of "current" or "common." It was not till 1590 that Pope Sixtus V called his edition the Vulgate of the Council of Trent: "By the fulness of apostolical power, we decree and declare that this edition of the sacred Latin Vulgate of the Old and New Testaments, which has been received as authentic by the Council of Trent . . . be received and held as true, legitimate, authentic, and unquestioned, in all public and private disputation, reading, preaching, and explanation." But the Pope died August 27, 1590, and, in spite of his anathemas, a new edition had to be issued in order to correct

ROMANCE AND TRAGEDY

the multitude of errors found in the book. Gregory makes merry over the fate of Bellarmin, who was refused canonization because he suggested the "pious fraud" of recalling the volume, making the corrections, and re-issuing it as if the deceased Sixtus had ordered it. They condemned Bellarmin, but did the very thing that he had suggested. The new edition appeared in 1592, and is called the Clementine Vulgate. And scholars are still at work on the "immaculate" text of the Latin Vulgate. Professor G. Henslow in 1909 published a volume entitled *The Vulgate the Source of False Doctrines* in which he undertakes "to show that it is in the Latin Vulgate that we shall discover the original source of most of the still remaining errors" (pp. 1 and 2). In particular (p. 4) he laments that sacerdotal terms are brought over into the N. T. from the O. T.

There were publishers of books and great libraries, before the days of Jerome. Pamphilus gathered a great ecclesiastical library in Cæsarea and was able to take an order from the Emperor Constantine for fifty fine Greek Bibles. Eusebius of Cæsarea carried on the work of Pamphilus. But in Alexandria there existed the greatest center of theological interest. Here Clement, a convert from Stoicism, succeeded Pantænus as head of the Catechetical School. He had a wide and rich literary culture, and quoted in his *Miscellanies* freely from Greek and Latin authors, Jewish and Christian. Mr. P. M. Barnard in *The Biblical Text of Clement of Alexandria* (1899) has shown that Clement used a type of text very much like the "Western" class of Westcott and Hort.

Clement of Alexandria was succeeded by a much greater scholar and critic, Origen. "In textual scholarship, indeed, Origen has no rival among ancient writers, and no single individual has exercised so wide an influence upon the Biblical text as he" (Kenyon, *Textual Criticism of the New Testament*, pp. 251 f.). He was only eighteen when he undertook this great task. He was driven out of Alexandria in 215, went to Cæsarea, and then returned to Alexandria in 219; and again in 231 he had trouble with his ecclesiastic overlords and made his home in Cæsarea till his death in 253. Thus Cæsarea had Origen, Pamphilus, Eusebius. Origen tells us why he preferred "Bethabara" to "Bethany" in John 1:28. He admitted that practically all the documents read "Bethany," but he could not find a Bethany beyond Jordan in his travels in Palestine, hence he preferred "Bethabara." That is subjective criticism with a vengeance. It is clear that such whimsical criticism existed very early. All the more do we wonder that we can restore a competently correct text of the N. T.

We pass by many centuries, silent and dark to us, but full of turmoil and labor for the patient monks who copied Greek and Latin manuscripts in the East and the West. Parchment (vellum), as we have seen, took the place of papyrus, and the codex supplanted the roll. Many of the vellum books are highly ornamented, and some are written in silver or gold on purple parchment. The minuscule or cursive hand displaced the beautiful but tedious uncial style. Finally paper came into use and printing. The first book to be printed was the Latin Vulgate at Mayence in 1455

ROMANCE AND TRAGEDY

(the Mazarin Bible). This was a significant fact, for Latin was now supreme in the West, and Greek was largely confined to the East. But the Renaissance came to the West with its revival of interest in Greek learning. The barbarians had nearly destroyed Greek culture and letters. The Arabs had kept the torch alive in the Far East. Now the West woke up with the Greek N. T. in its hands.

The hero of this epoch is Erasmus, the foremost classicist of his time. He did not indeed print the first Greek N. T. That honor belongs to Cardinal Francis Ximenes de Cisneros, Archbishop of Toledo and Prime Minister of Spain. This great Inquisitor was at work on a Polyglot Bible, called the Complutensian Polyglot, which was published in 1522 by the aid of Stunica, for Ximenes died in 1517. But the N. T. text was printed in 1514, over four hundred years ago, though not published till 1522. But Frobenius, of Basle, offered to pay Erasmus as much as anybody if he would get out a Greek N. T. before Ximenes published his polyglot. So Erasmus began to print his first edition of the Greek N. T., September 11, 1515, and finished it March 1, 1516. He won the race by six years, but at great cost to accuracy, and with lamentable results upon the history of the Greek N. T. He had five late minuscules at Basle. The best one (1) belonged to the eleventh century, and was so different from the others that Erasmus used it very little. Its text is very much like that of B and ℵ unknown to Erasmus. He had 2 (fifteenth century) for the Gospels, 2^{ap} (thirteenth or fourteenth century) for Acts and

Epistles, and 1ʳ (twelfth century) for the Apocalypse. The last one had a leaf missing at the end, and Erasmus retranslated the last six verses from the Latin Vulgate. "Some words of this re-translation from the Vulgate, which occur in no MS. whatever still linger in our Textus Receptus to the present day" (Kenyon, *Textual Criticism of the New Testament*, p. 269). Erasmus made a translation of the Greek into Latin, side by side with his Greek, and added sharp notes that greatly angered the ecclesiastics of Europe (see "The Romance of Erasmus's Greek Testament" in my *The Minister and his Greek New Testament*, 1923). The Greek N. T. of Erasmus sold like hot cakes, and laid the foundation of the Reformation of Luther and of Luther's German Bible and, sooth to say, of the Authorized English Version (King James). In the fourth edition of Erasmus (1527) he made some use of the Complutensian Polyglot, especially in the Apocalypse. But Erasmus remained technically a Roman Catholic, though denied honor at his funeral, and his body lies buried in the Protestant Minster at Basle.

If Erasmus had known that he was working for the ages, instead of getting ahead of Ximenes, he might have taken more pains to edit his Greek N. T. All his documents were late, and some were the poorest of the late ones. But soon Stephanus or Stephens (Estienne of Paris) issued his Greek N. T., which was mainly a reprint of the last edition of Erasmus (1527, 1535). His "royal edition" (*editio regia*) of 1550 became the main source for the Textus Receptus of England.

ROMANCE AND TRAGEDY

Beza prepared four editions (1565 to 1598) of the text of Stephens. He had the use of D and D$_2$, but "the time had not yet come for the safe operation of textual criticism" (Schaff, *Companion to the Greek Testament and English Version*, 1889, p. 238). So Beza let his chance slip to get back to an older text, but certainly D (Codex Bezæ) raises problems that trouble us still. The two last editions of Stephens, and the four of Beza, were those relied on chiefly for the Authorized English Version of 1611. It is impossible, therefore, to overestimate the importance of what Erasmus did in 1516.

But this is not all of the story. The Holland publishers, Bonaventure and Abraham Elzevir, republished Beza's edition of 1565 with the bald and bold claim: "*Textum ergo habes, nunc ab omnibus receptum: in quo nihil immutatum aut corruptum damus.*" This edition became the Textus Receptus for the Continent, as that of Stephens did for England. Schaff (*op. cit.* p. 241) puts the outcome pointedly: "The *textus receptus*, slavishly followed, with slight diversities, in hundreds of editions, and substantially represented in all the principal modern Protestant translations prior to the present century, thus resolves itself essentially into that of the last edition of Erasmus, formed from a few modern and inferior manuscripts and the Complutensian Polyglot, in the infancy of biblical criticism." That is tragedy, indeed, for the original Greek text which had travelled so long and so far to become fixed in this form! It has taken nearly four hundred years of the hardest kind of work to break that spell, and to go back to the older and the truer text.

At first men who wanted to get behind the Textus Receptus, like Fell and Mill, published the Elzevir or the Stephens text with variations of important manuscripts. Richard Bentley planned a new text on the basis of the oldest Greek and Latin manuscripts. He published his proposal, and it roused the hostility of all who were used to the Textus Receptus. Bentley was a fighter, but he died in 1742 before he published his text. Bengel was afraid to publish a text of his own. No publishers would risk the rage of the public. He made some changes in his text that had already appeared previously, but he made fine use of the margin with five classes of variants. Even this plan stirred so much hostility that he published in German and in Latin a "Defence of the Greek Testament" (1737). Wettstein (1751–2) did not dare to change the text of the Textus Receptus, but he published a fairly full critical apparatus which is still important for its numerous quotations from the early writers. He was also the first scholar to use capital letters for the uncial Greek manuscripts, and Arabic numbers for the minuscules. He was a poor critic, but a prodigious worker, and his N. T. is still indispensable as a storehouse of parallel passages from the Rabbinical writers and the classics. But he had a long and bitter controversy with two orthodox, but intolerant men, Iselin and Frey. His *Prolegomena* is full of this painful story.

Griesbach cut loose from the fetters of the Textus Receptus, and made the beginning of a really critical text. The edition of his N. T. ran from 1775 to 1807. He took hold of Bengel's system of families, and classified them as Western, Alexandrian, and Byzantine or

ROMANCE AND TRAGEDY

Constantinopolitan. Hort revered Griesbach more than any of his predecessors, and many of his canons of criticism are still used. He did not arouse as much antagonism as Bentley and Bengel had done.

But Lachmann's *Novum Testamentum Graece et Latine* (2 vols. 1842–1850) did meet with much opposition from the professional theologians. He was Professor of Classical Philology in Berlin, and even De Wette thought that he wasted his time and strength in trying to reproduce the text of the fourth century. He paid no attention to the late documents (Byzantine) and confined his attention to the Western and Alexandrian classes. "Such is the power of habit and prejudice that every inch of ground in the march of progress is disputed, and must be fairly conquered" (Schaff, *op. cit.*, p. 256).

Tregelles supplied a fairly full critical apparatus that followed in the line of Lachmann, but he was stricken with paralysis in 1870 while finishing the last chapters of Revelation. His *Prolegomena* was published four years after his death in 1875.

The work of Tischendorf is full of romance and tragedy. He was smitten with a stroke of apoplexy on May 5, 1873, and died December 7, 1874. He did not live to write the *Prolegomena* which was completed by Dr. Caspar René Gregory, an American scholar who gave himself to the task in Leipzig and completed it (1894). It is impossible to exaggerate the toils and travels of Tischendorf in behalf of a better text for the Greek N.T. His discovery of the Sinaitic manuscript (א) in the Monastery of St. Catherine on Mount Sinai is one of the most thrilling in all the range of research. He chanced in 1844 to notice in a waste-basket there some leaves of a codex that attracted his attention. They were ready to light the fire for the monks, as others had done. It took him fifteen years of patient diplomacy before he got hold of the rest of the precious ℵ, as he named it, a wonderful Greek Bible like B. This discovery and the publication of the *Facsimile* of B revolutionized Tischendorf's text in his eighth edition. That edition still has the best critical apparatus for the modern student. Gregory spent his life in getting ready to issue a new and up-to-date edition of Tischendorf's *Novum Testamentum Graece*, and then went to the front on behalf of Germany, though seventy years old, and fell on the firing line. That is tragedy indeed! And now we shall have to wait another generation for another young man to master this great field of research and make a new critical apparatus that will include all the new discoveries.

There is no tragedy about the work of Westcott and Hort, but only painstaking and triumphant success. They met the bitter opposition of able men like Burgon and Miller; and even Scrivener leaned to the Textus Receptus. But Hort was sure that he was on the right track, as the event has shown. Their principles still stand the test, though the new discoveries, like the Washington Codex and the Sinaitic Syriac, have given more value to the Western Text than Hort allowed. The Neutral Text still holds the field as the best that we know. Besides the critical text of Westcott and Hort, we have today the very similar text of Nestle and also of B. Weiss.

H. Von Soden adds another tragedy to the story by reason of his accidental death in a Berlin tube. He gave unremitting toil to a new system of notation that is very cumbersome, and not likely to displace that of Tischendorf as revised by Gregory. He also worked out a new system of families that challenges that used by Westcott and Hort, only much more complicated, and less satisfactory. But his Greek text (1913) does not differ radically from that of Westcott and Hort. It is an independent effort to find the best text, the one closest to the original.

It remains only to say that England was slow to take up the problem of printing the Bible for the people, but, once she did take hold, she has led the world. The ashes of Wycliffe, and then of Tindale, made a powerful appeal for the Bible in English. It is a sorrowful fact that the ecclesiastics of Britain brought the blood of these martyrs on their heads. God heard the prayer of Tindale as he was burned to death, October 6, 1536: "Lord, open the King of England's eyes." He did. The Authorized Version in 1611 was made at the request of King James. This wonderful translation was made from the Textus Receptus, with some help from the Latin Vulgate. It had a poor text, but it is marvellous English, and it lies at the foundation of Anglo-Saxon civilization. The Revised Version of 1881 is made from a better text, more like that of Westcott and Hort, but it can never play the part in Anglo-Saxon life that the Authorized Version has already performed.

Surely one is bound to thank God for the heroes who have struggled and triumphed through the centuries to give modern men an adequately correct text of the N. T. as we do have it today. With all the copyings, translations, and printings there is no heresy of moment in any manuscript or edition of the N. T. The Word of the Lord has run and been gloried through the ages, as Paul urged the Thessalonians to pray for his own preaching (2 Thess. 3:1).

CHAPTER III

HOW THE TEXTUS RECEPTUS WON ITS PLACE

All ministers and intelligent Christians in the English-speaking world know the powerful hold that the Authorized Version, published in 1611 under the auspices of King James, still has upon the masses of modern Christians. The reasons for this outstanding fact are various and strong. The story of the influence of the King James Version upon Anglo-Saxon civilization has often been told and cannot be told too often. A great library of books covers this wide and engaging theme. Men like Huxley, not Christians themselves, have freely acknowledged that this version of the Scriptures lies at the foundation of our liberty and of our progress. It is inwrought in our great literature and in the daily life of the humblest cottager. The music of its wonderful English lingers in our ears and its consummate phrases have comforted the struggling and the dying. British and American civilization rests upon the Bible, and among the masses that is still the Authorized Version. We have come upon a time when there is a spirit of resentment toward the Bible on the part of some. It is a good time to take stock of what the true situation is. In 1885 Philip Schaff wrote words about the Bible that apply today: "It rules from the pulpit, it presides at the family altar, it touches human life at every point from the cradle to the grave, and guides the soul on its lonely journey to the unseen world. It has molded the languages, laws, habits, and home-life of the nations of Europe, and inspired the noblest works of literature and art. The Bible retains with advancing age the dew and freshness of youth, and readapts itself in ever-improving versions to every age in every civilized land."[1]

This eloquent passage is not the language of mere emotion or of rhetoric. It is sober fact. It is true today in the full glare of the twentieth century with all the discoveries of science and of archæological research.

But the Authorized Version did not have it all its own way at first. The effort to give the Bible to the people of England is itself a story of martyrdom and of final triumph. The Roman Catholic Church resisted every attempt to give the Bible to the people. This powerful hierarchy destroyed Wycliffe and the Lollards and his translation from the Latin Vulgate. England was slow to wake up to the importance of the publication and circulation of the Bible. The first book published by the modern printing press was the Latin Vulgate (the Mazarin Bible) at Mayence in 1455. Latin was the ecclesiastical and literary language of Europe at that period. The first German Bible in the High German dialect was in 1462 and in the Low German dialect in 1480. But England lagged behind. The first edition of Tindale's English New Testament was printed on the Continent on the sly (first at Cologne and then at Worms) in 1525. It

[1] *"Companion to the Greek Testament and English Version,* page 306.

HOW THE TEXTUS RECEPTUS WON ITS PLACE

was secretly smuggled into England. But the Bishop of London, Dr. Tunstall, had as many copies as he could get his hands on publicly burned in St. Paul's churchyard not very far away from the Oxford Bible Warehouse in Paternoster Row and the Bible House of the British and Foreign Bible Society on the banks of the Thames. Dr. Warham, the Archbishop of Canterbury, bought up all the copies of Tindale's first edition that he could in order to keep them from circulation. But in doing that he also furnished the money for a new edition. God overrules the wrath of priests and prelates for his glory. Eadie[1] says that Tindale "caused the boy who driveth the plow to know more of the Scriptures than did all the priests."

The people had gotten a taste of the Word of God in their vernacular and it was not to be denied them by the jealousy of the Roman Catholic priesthood. It was the combination of the age of printing and the Renaissance with the Reformation of Luther that set the Bible loose in the languages of modern Europe. The reformers on the continent and in England were the first to see the power of the printing press in the circulation of the Bible. They kindled tremendous enthusiasm for the Word of God. They boldly placed the Bible to the front in their fight against papal oppression. "Foremost among the popular modern versions are the German, the Dutch, and the English. They have gained such a hold on the people that it is difficult to replace them by any new one, however superior it may be in accuracy."[2] The very zeal of

---

[1] *History of the English Bible*, Vol. I, page 129.
[2] Schaff, *op. cit.*, page 308.

the reformer for the circulation of the Bible among the people stiffened Roman opposition, which feared the power of the Bible and the spirit of freedom.

If England was slow in starting, the thing could not be stopped. Soon England took the lead and has never lost it. Tindale followed Wycliffe as martyr. He was strangled and burned at the stake on October 6, 1536, in the fortress of Vilvorde. In quick succession came the English Bible of Miles Coverdale (1535), Thomas Matthew (*alias* John Rogers, another martyr, 1537), Richard Taverner (1539), the Great Bible (1539), and the second with a preface by Archbishop Cranmer (1540), the Geneva Bible (1560), the Bishops' Bible (1568), and finally King James's Authorized Version (1611). It took from 1536 to 1604 for the eyes of the King of England to be fully opened, when he called the Revisers together, though they did not meet till 1607. The work was completed and published in 1611, but it had to win its way against all the other versions and was not free from errors of various kinds. But it did win its way at last and holds its grip on the masses even now.

But where does the Textus Receptus come in? The Textus Receptus is the Greek text that was translated into King James's Authorized Version as it had been into Luther's German Bible. These two great modern versions that have built two great modern civilizations were translated from the Greek text called the Textus Receptus.

What is the Textus Receptus? The phrase, it is worth repeating, comes from the second edition of the Greek New Testament in 1633 edited by the brothers

Bonaventure and Abraham Elzevir, who published it in Holland with unknown editors.

The Elzevir Greek New Testament, which became the Textus Receptus for the European continent, as already seen, was practically the same text as that of Stephens (since Beza copied Stephens), which was the Textus Receptus for England. So we must push our inquiry further back and find out what precisely was the Greek text of Robert Stephanus (or Stephens), the great printer and scholar of Paris. It was his "royal edition" (*editio regia*) in 1550 which became the standard for England and by means of Beza and Elzevir for the Continent. This third edition followed closely the editions of Erasmus of 1527 and 1535. "Already there seems to have arisen a fictitious worship for the letter of Erasmus's last edition, and often what is now regarded as unquestionably the right reading is to be found on Stephanus's inner margin, not in his text."[1] This is the first printed Greek New Testament that contains any critical apparatus, giving variations in readings by various manuscripts. There were fifteen Greek manuscripts that were used by Stephens, and nearly all of them can be identified today. Two of these manuscripts were the uncials D2 and L, but he made little use of them, just as Beza declined to make much use of D and D2. But Stephens also made marginal notes of certain readings in the Complutensian Polyglot, which was published in 1522. Robert Stephens is responsible for the introduction of the verse divisions into the Bible, his edition of the Latin Vulgate in 1555. But he had put them into his edition

[1] Souter, *Text and Canon of the New Testament*, page 96.

of the Greek New Testament for 1551, a reprint of the "royal edition" of 1550. "The versicular division is injudicious, and breaks up the text, sometimes in the middle of the sentence, into fragments, instead of presenting it in natural sections."[1] Stephens is reported to have made it on horseback from Paris to Lyons. Schaff is certain that the horse bumped so often that Stephens occasionally made the verse divisions in the wrong place. They are convenient to help preachers to find their texts, but they mar the sense and are a great hindrance to the understanding of the Bible.

So then it all comes back to Erasmus. But what sort of a Greek text was that published by Erasmus that was destined to shape the text of the world for hundreds of years and to become almost an object of worship for some? The German New Testament, the Dutch New Testament, and the English New Testament go back straight to the Greek New Testament of Erasmus. It is a curious thing about the so-called Textus Receptus that no two editions are precisely alike. The changes are numerous, but usually of minor importance. "The text of Erasmus, with various changes and improvements of Stephens, Beza, and the Elzevirs, assumed a stereotyped character and acquired absolute dominion among scholars."[2] Erasmus did his work in such haste that, though he began to print on September 11, 1515, it was finished by March 1, 1516. Erasmus praised his own work in a letter to the pope, but later admitted that "it was done

---

[1] Schaff, *op. cit.*, page 237.
[2] Schaff, *op. cit.*, page 228.

HOW THE TEXTUS RECEPTUS WON ITS PLACE 49

headlong rather than edited." It was printed at Basle, Switzerland, and appeared just one year before the Reformation. Desiderius Erasmus was a great scholar for his time and was a leader in the Renaissance. He was the bearer of the torch of Greek learning to Luther, but let Luther carry the torch on to victory while he withdrew from the contest. He gave Tindale and Luther the Greek text for their vernacular translations, which were the great levers of the Reformation and helped the people to throw off the Roman yoke. Erasmus printed a Latin translation of the Greek text with notes in which he made pointed jibes at the inconsistencies of the priests. This fact angered the ecclesiastics, but made his Greek Testament a best seller. The more it was attacked, the more it was bought and read. The pope continued to be his friend and even offered him a cardinal's hat, which he declined. But the Sorbonne in 1527 solemnly condemned thirty-two items from the works of Erasmus. He died without a priest and his body is buried in the Protestant Minster of Basle. But in his way he did a great deal to help on the revolution started by the Renaissance and the Reformation.

He had only a few Greek manuscripts from which to print his Greek New Testament. The publisher's preface says that he used many ancient manuscripts. As a matter of fact, they were not old and they were not good. One can see at a glance that such a printed Greek New Testament has no critical value at all. In 1519 Erasmus issued a revised edition which corrected many misprints, but even this edition is said to contain several pages of errors which have affected

Luther's German version of the New Testament. In 1522 Erasmus brought out the third edition, which contains the spurious passage about the three heavenly witnesses in 1 John 5: 7, 8: "In heaven, the Father, the Word, and the Holy Ghost: and these three are one. And there are three that bear witness in earth." These words Erasmus could not find in any Greek manuscript and so did not put them in his first and second editions. But Ximenes had them in his Complutensian Polyglot, and Stunica, who carried on the work of Ximenes after his death, in 1517, chided Erasmus sharply for not having the words in his Greek Testament. In a moment of rashness Erasmus promised that if any one could produce a Greek manuscript containing the passage, he would insert it. Accordingly he was presented with a sixteenth-century minuscule Greek manuscript with the passage. The thing looked suspicious to Erasmus and he suspected that some one had translated the passage from a Latin Vulgate manuscript on purpose to make him print it in his third edition of 1522. That manuscript with this forged passage is now in Dublin. Erasmus stood by his promise and printed it. It is now known that Erasmus was absolutely right in his suspicion of the passage. Cyprian had interpreted the real text as referring to the Trinity, and Priscillian and others had taken it up as part of the text so that the Vulgate manuscript had it. This is not the only error in the Greek New Testament of Erasmus, but it is the outstanding one. In his fourth edition of 1527 Erasmus made some use of the Complutensian Polyglot which was published in 1522. In the book of Revelation

HOW THE TEXTUS RECEPTUS WON ITS PLACE

he made a number of improvements in the text by the use of the Polyglot text. In this edition, besides the Greek text and his Latin translation, he gave also the text of the Latin Vulgate in a third parallel column. So this was his definitive text, that of 1527. The fifth and last edition of 1535 was just a reprint with the omission of the Latin Vulgate text. The Textus Receptus in the main was derived from these two last editions of the Greek New Testament of Erasmus.

It was thus that the text of the Textus Receptus got its start. It was Erasmus and Stephens in England. It was Erasmus, Stephens, Beza, Elzevir on the Continent. But it was mainly the text of Erasmus. We have seen how the use of *textum receptum* by the Elzevirs in their edition of 1633 led to the adoption of the phrase for the Received Text. "These ignorant words are what did the mischief, and led to two centuries of trouble for textual critics. It was not the case that that was the text received by all, and much less was it the text that should have been received by all. But people, even many who should have known better, whose education should have enabled them to free themselves from the limitations of these publishers, clung to these words, busied themselves with the effort to prove them true, and denounced all who did not agree with them at least as blinded, but sometimes as traitors to the truth, destroyers of the New Testament, and it may be as totally immoral and detestable persons."[1] Tradition quickly gathers strength and hardens into a crust.

The text of Erasmus, therefore, was printed from a

[1] Gregory, *The Canon and Text of the New Testament*, page 444.

few very late and very poor minuscules and it was crudely and hastily printed. The one good manuscript that Erasmus had, the minuscule 1, which agrees with the text of the best early uncials now known (Codex Sinaiticus and Codex Vaticanus), Erasmus was afraid to use. If he had printed carefully the Greek text of this one good manuscript, a good deal of trouble would have been spared scholars and preachers. But, once the poor and late Greek text of Erasmus got its grip on the world, it has taken the strength of titans in scholarship and four hundred years of struggle to shake loose its hold. Scholars in the sphere of textual criticism have fought their way slowly back toward the early and the best text obtainable by means of the comparatively few early documents as opposed to the many and late manuscripts full of corruptions.

The modern English translations of the New Testament (Canterbury, American Standard, Weymouth, Twentieth Century, Moffatt's, Riverside, Goodspeed's, Mrs. Montgomery's) are all made from the modern critical text, not from the Textus Receptus. In time people will come to understand that textual critics of the New Testament have not been robbing them of the New Testament. They have been trying to restore to them the original Greek text as far as it is possible to do so with all the resources of modern discovery and modern knowledge. Today critics have photographic facsimiles of the great primary uncials (Codex Sinaiticus, Codex Alexandrinus, Codex Vaticanus, Codex Ephraemi Rescriptus, Codex Bezæ, Codex Washingtonius). The whole modern science of textual criticism has been worked out by Hort so that men can now

HOW THE TEXTUS RECEPTUS WON ITS PLACE

handle the great mass of manuscripts with some skill and confidence. It is no longer accident or chance or guesswork. "The *Textus Receptus* is as dead as Queen Anne." [1] Cambridge was the home of Lightfoot, Westcott, and Hort, as Oxford was the home of Sanday. We owe the modern critical text chiefly to these great universities, especially Cambridge. And yet in *Cambridge Biblical Essays* for 1909, page 512, Prof. Valentine-Richards says of the text of Erasmus, Stephens, Elzevir, the Textus Receptus: "It was reproduced with conscientious care by the late Dr. Scrivener, and his edition is still being reprinted by the University Press at Cambridge, while the slightly revised version of Estienne's third edition, published by Mill at the Clarendon Press in 1707, is still the standard in the sister university." But all the same Professor C. H. Turner of Oxford is right. The Textus Receptus is as dead as Queen Anne. No one now turns to it in any real argument any more than one turns to the Authorized Version for any crucial matter of text. In any pinch one wants the truth, the real text, if he can get it. No one thinks that Westcott and Hort have been able to reproduce the original Greek text at every point. But they have left the Textus Receptus so far behind that it is hopelessly out of the running. Research will go on and no trouble will be wasted that will help us get closer to the autograph copies of the books of the New Testament.

[1] Turner, *The Study of the New Testament*, page 49.

CHAPTER IV

WHY TEXTUAL CRITICISM FOR THE PREACHER

To the average preacher there is no more uninteresting or uninviting field of study than the textual criticism of the New Testament. Many do not even know the meaning of the phrase. It is not taught in all our theological seminaries. I once asked a graduate of one of the leading American theological schools if he had studied textual criticism in his course of training. He said that he had had it in homiletics. He betrayed such a blissful ignorance of the theme that I did not have the courage to disillusion him.

Some ministers still betray a certain amount of exasperation over the subject and hold a kind of grudge against Westcott and Hort who have robbed them of some of their favorite texts like John 5:4 with the story of the periodic visit of the angel to the pool of Bethesda, Acts 8:37 with the confession of the Eunuch, 1 John 5:7 and 8 with its clear statement of the doctrine of the Trinity. I well recall as a college student the irritation of various ministers, when in 1881 the Canterbury Revision appeared. It made a great sensation, for one of the New York dailies printed it in full. The ministers, who objected, preferred the wonderful English of the Authorized Version, as many people of culture do still, including Professor William

Lyon Phelps of Yale University. But there were others more like the old preacher who said that the King James Version was good enough for the Apostle Paul and it was good enough for him.

Others objected to the new text that lay behind the Canterbury Revision (and the American Standard Version). They had come to feel that the *Textus Receptus*, the Greek text from which the Authorized Version was made, was the original text and they did not want to see it tampered with. They felt that some scholars were trying to rob them of parts of the New Testament. Drs. Burgon and Miller made a vigorous protest against the text of Westcott and Hort and so of the Revisers. The fight of Burgon and Miller was made with great ability and earnestness and not without much learning. But it was a losing fight and it is now lost for good. At bottom Westcott and Hort are right. Hort never answered Burgon, not because he could not do so, but because he preferred for the facts that he had produced to speak for themselves. He knew that he could afford to wait and that the truth would win in the end.

It is not here claimed that the text of Westcott and Hort is correct at every point. After all, the text which they print is simply their opinion of the correct text in the light of all the evidence. But it is opinion regulated by a scientific view of all the data that has, in its main outline, stood the test of time.

The intelligent minister today cannot afford to remain in complete ignorance of this subject. If he does, he may find himself preaching from a text that some of the Sunday School teachers may know is not genuine. Or he may be unable to form an intelligent opinion on the point at issue and have to rely wholly upon the opinions of others. Few things are more dreary than pulpit quotations of scholars on any given point, whether *pro* or *con*.

It is impossible for the preacher to escape the issues of New Testament textual criticism. In Luke 2:14 shall he say "men of goodwill" or "goodwill among men"? In Matthew 6:13, shall he use the Doxology as a part of the text? In Matthew 6:4 and 6 shall he use the words "openly" or not? In John 7:8, did Jesus say "I go not up" or "I go not yet up"? In John 9:4, shall we read "We must work the works of him that sent me," "We must work the works of him that sent us," or "I must work the works of him that sent me"? In John 7:53–8:11 what shall we do about the story of the woman taken in adultery? Did Mark end his Gospel at 16:8 or not? In Romans 5:1, did Paul write, "We have peace," "Let us make peace," or "Let us keep on having peace?" In 1 Timothy 3:16, did Paul write "God manifest in the flesh," "Which was manifest in the flesh," or "Who was manifest in the flesh"? Did Paul leave out "at Ephesus" in Ephesians 1:1? In John 1:18, did John write "Only begotten Son," or "Only begotten God"? These instances are sufficient to show how important the subject of textual criticism is to the minister.

It is a technical study, but it can be first approached from the popular side. Paterson Smyth's *How We Got Our Bible* is a fascinating little book and it will introduce one to the beginnings of the topic, as well as to the study of the canon, a different subject. Cobern's *New Archaeological Discoveries in Their Bearing on the New Testament* will also prepare one in a helpful way to later interest in the further study of the subject. If one has read thus far, he will certainly desire to go further. The simplest and clearest little handbook on the subject is that by Kirsopp Lake, now of Harvard University, called *The Text of the New Testament* (108 pages). It is one of the Oxford Church Text Books and gives the gist of the matter in a way that the reader can understand, even without a teacher. But one who wishes to get a firm grasp on the theme will wish to do more.

There are other books that one can read like Souter's *The Text and Canon of the New Testament* (pages 1 to 145 on the Text, and it is done with great ability and judgment), Kenyon's *Handbook to the Textual Criticism of the New Testament* (pages 1 to 379, but up to 313 devoted to a full and accurate discussion of the material and history of textual criticism), Nestle's *Introduction to the Textual Criticism of the New Testament* (with many details of value about the manuscripts), and Gregory's *Canon and Text of the New Testament* (pages 297 to 539 on the Text and written in a lively and captivating style). Gregory's discussion is non-technical, though written by the modern master of the subject. What Gregory has here written will serve splendidly to whet one's appetite for the more technical discussions by Lake, Nestle, Souter and Kenyon. A popular manual is Schaff's *Companion to the Greek Testament and the English Versions*. No real student can afford to neglect B. H. Streeter's *The Four Gospels*

(1925). I have, myself, written an *Introduction to the Textual Criticism of the New Testament* (1925) a book that is designed as a text-book for class use. I have taught the subject for a generation and have never taught anything that created more interest among the men of scholarly instincts and training. The men get a sense of satisfaction in learning how to deal with the sources of our knowledge concerning the text of the New Testament that is gratifying in the extreme.

I have given this list of modern books about the subject in the hope that many ministers who read this chapter may be stimulated to revive their knowledge if they ever knew anything about it, and also with the desire to stir some up to take hold of it if they know nothing about it. Even if one does not become an expert in it, he will gain a sense of independence in reaching probable conclusions that will be satisfying.

Dr. John A. Broadus was exceedingly fond of teaching textual criticism. He used to say that it came nearer to being an exact science than anything else in New Testament study. One feels that his feet are striking solid rock. He is not simply up in the air of speculative theory.

There is also a splendid training in clear thinking in this study. One balances the various forms of evidence before he reaches a final conclusion. This mental process calls for insight, weighing evidence, delicate balancing of probabilities, clear grasp of all the data, honesty in deciding. These qualities are not confined, to be sure, to this study, but they are so demanded by it that one gains a fine intellectual drill in the exercise of them.

TEXTUAL CRITICISM FOR THE PREACHER

I am well aware of the fact that most ministers are busy men and many of them find it difficult to get time for the necessary sermon preparation. But it will pay any preacher to cut short some of his light reading and add to his intellectual pabulum by a stiff brush, now and then, with the text of the New Testament.

To be sure, one will need the two volumes of Tischendorf's *Novum Testamentum Graece* (eighth edition) if he wishes to have the best apparatus for his work. These two volumes are indispensable for one to be able to have the full information before him on any passage. Many of the critical commentaries give some of the important readings in the leading manuscripts, but they do not undertake to give them all.

Some younger man will, doubtless, begin to get ready for Gregory's unfinished task. He wrote many books, but not the book for which he had toiled for a lifetime. Interest in the subject cannot be allowed to die out because Gregory was killed. The subject is too vital for all who love Christ and also love the New Testament for no further progress to be made in it.

It is not claimed that the autograph text of the New Testament has been restored. The original copies perished long ago, but it is true that the critical text of Westcott and Hort is far closer to the original than the text printed by Erasmus. He had only a half dozen late Greek manuscripts. Today over four thousand Greek manuscripts of portions of the New Testament are known and new ones are discovered year by year. The very wealth of new material now available makes it possible to approximate the original text of the New Testament with an accuracy not possible for any ancient author — where conjecture has to play so large a part because of the paucity of evidence for the text.

In the study of the textual criticism of the New Testament no notice is taken of printed editions of the Greek New Testament, of which over a thousand have appeared. These merely reproduce what is already in Greek manuscripts which are still in existence. The printed Greek New Testaments are simply the opinions of the editors as to what the text is and are based on Greek manuscripts or upon other printed Greek New Testaments. They are therefore collusive and superfluous testimony for the real text. Only manuscripts are employed in the search for the original text.

These manuscripts may be in Greek or in some other language. If they are copies of the Greek New Testament, they naturally have more interest than translations into Syriac, Coptic, or Latin. But early translations can be of great help as showing whether a passage was in existence at an early date. Quotations from early writers (Fathers) help also to give the date of a given reading. These quotations are often rather free, as sometimes now with preachers, and the same writer frequently quotes a text in several ways.

The manuscripts of the Greek New Testament are divided into uncials (inch-size letters written separately) and minuscules or cursives where the letters run together as in our script. These letters are smaller than the uncials, which are more like a child's print letters. The tenth century is the broad general division between the two styles, though minuscules occur in the ninth and uncials as late as the eleventh.

Many of these Greek New Testaments, both uncial and cursive, are very beautiful and exhibit great skill in penmanship. In the uncials the letters are separate, but the words are not. They run together in a solid stream, and to read aloud one of Paul's epistles, for instance, called for a trained eye.

The very multitude of the witnesses for the Greek New Testament called for system in the use of the material. Most of the four thousand Greek manuscripts are minuscules and date from the ninth century on, most of them quite late. If mere numbers are to count, the later text will carry the day because it has the most witnesses. Most of the early manuscripts perished in the wholesale destruction due to the persecutions by the Roman emperors and to the ravages of the Goths and Vandals. It is wholly uncritical to decide a reading by the majority vote of the documents. One early Greek uncial on a given point may be right against the whole mass of minuscules.

But it is not only the text of the oldest documents that we want today. We desire to get the true text, the original text as far as it is possible to do so. It is not simply an old text that is wanted. Some errors in the text are very early, almost as old as any known document. Copyists knew how to make blunders in the second century as well as in the tenth or the fifteenth. The difference is that scribes in the fifteenth or the sixteenth century had so many possible copyings behind them that the chances for blunders are much greater in the later centuries.

The great work of Westcott and Hort is precisely this, that they used the advances made by Griesbach,

Lachmann, Tregelles, and others before them to develop a scientific method of handling the vast material at the disposal of modern scholars. Most of this material is made available by Tischendorf in the eighth edition of his *Novum Testamentum Graece* (2 vols.) and by Gregory's *Prolegomena* to that edition. Hort applied both external and internal evidence to any reading that was disputed as shown by the documents.

Internal evidence is both transcriptional and intrinsic. Transcriptional evidence looks at the problem, like John 5:4, from the standpoint of the scribe. Which is more likely, that the scribe would add it or omit it? Intrinsic evidence looks at it from the standpoint of the author. Which reading suits the context best? Usually these two lines of evidence agree. Sometimes they disagree.

But Hort applied this same method to a whole document like the manuscript B or D and reached a conclusion about each document as about a single reading. Then he took up groups of documents and found the value of many of these.

But the discovery that there were four classes or families of documents has done more than anything else to give help in the use of these documents. The names of the four classes are Syrian, Neutral, Alexandrian, Western. The Syrian is the latest of them all and made use of the three pre-Syrian classes (Neutral, Alexandrian, Western), as is shown by conflate readings where the Neutral had one reading, the Western another, the Syrian both (combining them). Hence it follows that any reading that is solely Syrian is wrong, because it is later than the pre-Syrian reading or readings. The Syrian class is found in late uncials, the mass of minuscules, late versions, and late writers (Fathers). It is easy to detect. The Western class is represented by the Codex Bezæ (D) in the Gospels and Acts, the Old Syriac, the Old Latin, Irenæus, Tertullian, and Cyprian, with occasional support of other documents. The Neutral class is found mainly in the Codex Vaticanus (B), the Codex Sinaiticus (Aleph), the Bohairic (Coptic) Version, Origen, with occasional support from Codex Alexandrinus (A), Codex Washingtonius (W), the Latin Vulgate, and the best of the minuscules. The Alexandrian class is a branch from the stock from which the Neutral comes and has no constant representatives. As a matter of fact, the Alexandrian class usually agrees with the Neutral or with the Western class. When the Alexandrian class stands alone, it is always wrong. The documents that most frequently give Alexandrian readings are C, L, Δ, W, Origen, Cyril.

In point of fact, the real contest is between the Neutral and the Western classes. As a rule the Neutral class is right as against the Western which has many additions and whimsical readings. But occasionally the Western class is right, especially in what Hort called Western non-interpolations which is only another way of saying Neutral interpolations like the insertion of John 19:34 after Matt. 27:49.

In simple truth, no single document now known is free from blunders of some sort. No one of the four classes is always right. The two oldest classes, the Neutral and the Western, go back to the third century and possibly to the end of the second. But it cannot be claimed that either of them at all points accurately reproduces the original text. However, the area of errors is reduced to exceedingly small proportions and is not enough to worry any serious mind. The marvel is that through all the centuries of repeated copying by so many men in so many languages the text of the New Testament has suffered so little real damage. We may be sure that nothing essential has been lost.

New discoveries constantly give zest to the search for the original text. Tischendorf's own story of his discovery of Aleph in the Convent of St. Catherine on Mount Sinai is as fascinating as a novel. This manuscript belongs to the fourth century A.D., like the Codex Vaticanus, and is only second in value to it. Mrs. A. S. Lewis and her sister, Mrs. M. D. Gibson, discovered also in the same convent the Sinaitic Syriac manuscript of the gospels which has cleared up the dispute about the Old Syriac Version and is closely allied to the Curetonian Syriac. Americans take special pride in the fact that the Washington Manuscript (W) in the Smithsonian Institution is one of the six primary uncials of the gospels. Mr. C. L. Freer, of Detroit, purchased this valuable document (which belongs probably to the fifth century) in Egypt and brought it to this country. It has a mixed text, now one class, now the other, though rather frequently Neutral.

It is plain that no intelligent minister can afford to be indifferent to the textual criticism of the New Testament. The subject fascinates those who study it long enough to feel at home in it, and it repays amply all the work that one may devote to it.

CHAPTER V

LOSSES AND GAINS IN THE CRITICAL TEXT OF THE NEW TESTAMENT

It is now over forty years since the Canterbury Revision in 1881 made a sensation in the theological and the literary world. It was not merely the new translation of familiar passages that excited interest and even alarm, but the new text employed by the Revision Committee. In 1882 Westcott and Hort published their now famous *New Testament in the Original Greek*. This text had been at the service of the committee in the Jerusalem Chamber. Not all the changes found in the new text of Westcott and Hort were adopted by the learned committee who made the Canterbury Revision. The actual text which they followed can be found in Palmer's *The Greek Testament* (1881). He gives the readings adopted by the Revisers of the Authorized Version. At the foot of each page he gives the readings of the Textus Receptus ("Received Text") which have been displaced. Weymouth in 1892 published what he called *The Resultant Greek Testament*. He gives the text in which the majority of modern scholars are agreed, including Stephens (1550), Lachmann, Tregelles, Tischendorf, Lightfoot, Ellicott, Alford, Weiss, Westcott and Hort, and the Revision Committee. In footnotes he gives the differences between the editors named. Whitney in two volumes (1891) has discussed *The Revisers' Greek Text*. Scrivener in 1881 published *The New Testament in the Original Greek* which was the Textus Receptus with the variations adopted in the Revised Version. But the best edition for getting the Greek text of the revisers is that of Souter, *Novum Testamentum Graece* (1909). In footnotes he gives a brief critical apparatus which makes it exceedingly useful. One will find it useful also to compare the text of the New Testament edited by B. Weiss and the one produced on new lines by H. von Soden (1913) with brief critical apparatus.

There was violent opposition to the Greek text of Westcott and Hort by Dean J. W. Burgon and Dr. E. Miller. It was once considered strange, as already noted, that Dr. Hort, who wrote the *Introduction* (Vol. II. of *The New Testament in the Original Greek*), never replied to the onslaughts of Dr. Burgon, who was a very able man. Burgon studied a great deal in the manuscripts and early writers and he struck hard blows at the new text of Westcott and Hort. He made an impression on a portion of the public, but not upon Dr. Hort, who went serenely on his way in full confidence that he was on the right track and that time would prove it so. He felt that his work spoke for itself. Burgon's *Revision Revised* was violent and extreme. It may be recalled that the Authorized Version of 1611 was accused of atheism and popery. When Jerome translated the Bible into Latin in 405, later called the Vulgate, he encountered such bitter opposition that he lost his temper and called his opponents

LOSSES AND GAINS IN THE CRITICAL TEXT 67

bipedes asellos, and possibly some of them were. Burgon did not provoke Hort to say anything like that.

But water enough has now run under the mill for us to be able to look at the critical text of the Revisers and of Westcott and Hort with less heat than was possible at first. No scholars of special importance now seriously contend for the Textus Receptus. Hort has certainly won his contention with the critics who are competent to pass judgment on the rival texts. And yet few today would insist that Hort is correct in all points. The new discoveries, particularly the Sinaitic Syriac and the Washington Manuscript (W). have thrown new light on the text of the Gospels, The Western text, especially as opposed to Neutral interpolations, Hort's "Western noninterpolations," ranks higher than it did with Hort. But the Neutral text still far outweighs the Western text on the whole. Certainly Hort followed the Vatican manuscript (B) too closely as when he put into the margin the preposition for "under" with the lampstand in Mark 4:21. This is a mere mechanical blunder. One is at a loss likewise to understand why he thought it worth while to put at the end of Matthew 27:49 the narrative about the piercing of the body of Jesus before his death. It is so manifestly a crude harmonistic error copied from John 19:34 where it is genuine and in the right place. The Western class is here right against the Neutral class. Hort expresses the opinion by double brackets that the insertion is not genuine in Matthew 27:49. He should not have burdened his text with it at all.

Perhaps the omission of 1 John 5:7 and 8, the

passage about the Trinity, in the Revised Version gave more offence at first than any other single thing. Some critics acted as if the doctrine of the Trinity hinged on this spurious passage. Today it seems surprising that so much importance was attached to these words, for the doctrine of the Trinity does not depend upon their genuineness. Certainly, no one today who believes in the Trinity wants the doctrine supported by a false passage like this. It is a great gain to have it out since Erasmus, as previously explained, was tricked into inserting it in his third edition (1522).

Another passage, 1 Timothy 3:16, gave almost equal offence when the Revised Version followed the lead of Westcott and Hort and put "he who" in the place of "God." The change in this passage coupled with that in 1 John 5:7 and 8 induced some to say that the Revisers were really Unitarians. This charge was an absurd one in the face of the fact that the leading spirits were men like Bishop Ellicott, Bishop Lightfoot, Bishop Westcott, and Dr. Hort. But these men had the courage to translate the true text, as far as they could find it, and not just the traditional text, the Textus Receptus. The evidence as given by Tischendorf in his *Novum Testamentum Graece* (8th edition) is very interesting. There are three readings. All the evidence for "God" (*theos* in the Greek) is late and belongs to the Syrian class of documents (late Greek manuscripts, late versions, late Fathers). But there are two pre-Syrian readings, both of which are relatives. One of these (Greek *ho*) is neuter singular and agrees in grammatical gender with the preceding word *musterion* (our "mystery"). This reading is supported by the Western class of documents which is sometimes right, but usually wrong when opposed to the Neutral class. The other reading and the right one is the relative pronoun also, but in the masculine gender (Greek *hos*). This reading is supported by the Neutral and Alexandrine classes, the two remaining classes of documents which often agree. The Vatican Manuscript (B) is wanting in this part of the New Testament, but the other Neutral documents are on this side. The evidence works out as follows: All the pre-Syrian classes reject "God" in favor of "who" or "which." A reading that is only Syrian always turns out to be wrong. But this is not all. Tischendorf quotes a passage from Liberatus, archdeacon of Carthage about 554 A.D., who says that Macedonius was expelled by the Emperor Anastasius for changing "who" to "God" in this passage, turning *omikron* to *theta*. It is not known whether this was the origin of the reading "God" or not. Others may have mistaken the Greek uncial *omikron* for the Greek uncial *theta*. The point of it all is that the reading "who" accounts for both of the others and is undoubtedly genuine. The disagreement in grammatical gender is a small matter, because the agreement is in sense (natural gender). It is even possible that Paul is here quoting from an early Christian hymn concerning the incarnation of Christ. Once more, it should be said that the deity of Jesus Christ does not rest upon a proof-text where the word "God" was inserted for the purpose of making a proof-text.

It may be reassuring to some to know that the

trend of modern knowledge of the text of the New Testament has not been all against the deity of Christ in actual statement. In John 1:18 the Revised Version (both Canterbury and American) follows the Authorized Version in giving "the only begotten Son." Westcott and Hort here restore "God only begotten" to the text because these words are supported by the Neutral and Alexandrian classes whereas "the only begotten Son" is given only by Western and Syrian documents. At bottom the issue turns on the relative merit of the Neutral and the Western classes of documents which are here in opposition. The decision goes to the Neutral unless there is something in the internal evidence (transcriptional or intrinsic) to turn the scale to the Western side. That is not the case, because the average scribe would more likely be disturbed by the words "God only begotten" than by "the only begotten Son." As a matter of fact, however, there is nothing in "God only begotten" not already in John 1:1 ("the Word was God") and 1:14 ("the Word became flesh"). By this reading verse 18 simply joins together the two statements previously made about the Deity and the incarnation of the Logos. But the Revisers were not ready to follow the lead of Westcott and Hort on this point, since the decision was reached by majority vote, not always on the merit of the argument.

In Acts 20:28 it is only the American Committee (American Standard Version) which gives us "the church of the Lord which he purchased with his own blood." The Neutral class here reads "God" against "Lord" in the Western and Alexandrian. The late

Syrian documents have a conflate reading, "Lord and God," combining both readings. Hort is certain that "God" is correct here. It is certainly the hard reading and would naturally lead to change. But it does make sense. Hort thinks that it is possible that the word "Son" has dropped out after "his own," "by the blood of his own Son." It is possible that this is Paul's meaning even without "Son," that is that it is God's blood through his Son. That is a possible meaning if one is not willing to admit that Paul ever applied the word "God" to Christ. In favor of that position there remains the natural punctuation in Romans 9:5 and the obvious meaning in Titus 2:13. In this latter passage the Authorized Version has "the great God and our Saviour Jesus Christ" but the Canterbury Revision puts it rightly "our great God and Saviour Jesus Christ." The American Committee, however, returned to the Authorized Version rendering. This wrong translation is not due to a difference in text, but to a failure to see the significance of the one article with both words, God and Saviour, in apposition with Jesus Christ. This argument is explained in detail in my book on *The Minister and His Greek New Testament* (chapter on "The Greek Article and the Deity of Christ").

The Revisers did not hesitate to omit various small additions that had crept into the text, like "openly" in Matthew 6:4, 6, an Alexandrian and Syrian addition to make it correspond with "in secret." Likewise the repetition of Mark 9:48 (supported here by all classes) in verses 44 and 46 by the Western and Syrian classes is rejected by the Neutral and Alexandrian classes. The Revised Version follows Westcott and Hort in leaving out these two verses. In John 5: 4 we lose in the Revised Version the story of the angel disturbing the water. It is an evident interpolation to explain the word "disturbed" in verse 7. It is supported by the Alexandrian and Syrian classes with some Western documents. But it is rejected by the Neutral class and most of the Western documents. The Revised Version retains it in a footnote, but it is certainly not genuine. In like manner we miss Acts 8: 37 which the Revised Version puts in a footnote. It is a Western addition probably due to ecclesiastical custom in baptizing. The Revisers also follow Westcott and Hort in omitting the addition to 1 Cor. 6: 20 "and in your spirit, which are his." This is a Syrian addition evidently made to take some of the burden off the body. But Paul is here specifically urging his readers to glorify God in the body.

Probably Christians have missed the Doxology from the Lord's Prayer in Matthew 6: 13 more than any of the other omission from the Authorized Version. The Revised Version gives it in the margin. Westcott and Hort reject it. The Neutral and Western classes combine against it. It does appear in some early Western documents in a shorter form and differing from each other. The Alexandrian and Syrian classes give it with some Western documents. Several of the early Christian writers have it, but each one again in a different form. Its origin was manifestly liturgical. It is harmless, but not a real part of the Lord's Prayer.

In 1 Cor. 11: 24 the Authorized Version has "which is broken for you." The Revised Version has only "which is for you" according to the text of Westcott and Hort. The Syrian class has "broken" after a few Western documents. Other Western documents have "which is given for you," as in Luke 22:19. The Neutral and Alexandrian classes read simply "which is for you." This is clearly right and the explanation of the others. Probably "given" was first inserted from Luke. Then it was changed to "broken" because Jesus "broke" the bread. But, as a matter of fact, the body of Jesus was not "broken" because he was dead already (John 19:33) before the soldier pierced his side. But it is rarely the case that one does not hear the Scripture quoted thus: "This is my body, which is broken for you." But this is not the text nor is it the fact.

The Revised Version follows Westcott and Hort in reading "Bethany" instead of "Bethabarah" in John 1:28. The Neutral class and most of the Western documents read Bethany. The Alexandrian class and some few of the Western documents have Bethabarah. The Syrian documents are also divided. The interesting thing about this reading is the fact that Origen tells that he himself changed the reading of the ancient manuscripts from Bethany to Bethabarah. He had made a visit to Palestine and found no Bethany beyond Jordan, but only the one near Jerusalem. So he changed the name in the face of the documents. This is the kind of scholarly correction that marks the Alexandrian class and Origen is one of the leading witnesses for it.

Another passage of interest is that in John 9:4. The Revised Version follows Westcott and Hort here in reading: "We must work the works of him that sent me." This is the reading of the Neutral class with some Western support. The Alexandrian class has: "We must work the works of him that sent us." The Syrian class follows some Western documents in reading: "I must work the works of him that sent me." The Western documents are often divided and represent different strata of evidence. But it is clear here that the Neutral class is right and that Jesus here associates his disciples with him in the work that God gave him. The Alexandrian class changed the second "me" to "us." The Syrian, preceded by some Western documents, changed the first "us" to "I." The Authorized Version follows the Syrian class as usual with "I" and "me."

People have not yet gotten used to the new text in Luke 2:14 "men of good will" instead of "good will among men." But there is nothing clearer in textual criticism than this passage. The Neutral and Western classes combine in reading "men of good will" and they only unite in the autograph copy. The Alexandrian class changed the genitive here (*eudokias*) to the nominative (*eudokia*) by dropping *s*, one letter only. The true text means men who are the subjects of God's good will.

There is little protest made now to the relegation of John 7:53–8:11 to a footnote as in the Revised Version. Westcott and Hort print it at the end of the Gospel of John on a separate page. It is wanting in the Neutral and Alexandrian classes and appears in the Western and Syrian classes. A few manuscripts put it at the close of the Gospel of John and

LOSSES AND GAINS IN THE CRITICAL TEXT 75

some at the end of Luke 21. It is probably a true incident, for it is wondrously like Jesus to act as he did toward this sinful woman. But it is not a part of the Gosepl of John.

There is no space left to discuss the disputed ending of Mark's gospel, 16: 9–20. The Washington Manuscript adds a passage after verse 14 not in other documents. A few documents give a still shorter ending, but the Neutral class has no ending. I have discussed the problem in detail in the closing chapter of my *Studies in Mark's Gospel*. It may be added here that the common ending is probably due to Aristion, mentioned by Papias, and is in fact mainly a summary of Matthew 28. It is hardly probable that Mark ended his Gospel at verse 8. The last leaf may have been torn off or Mark may have been interrupted. Doctor Caspar René Gregory even hoped that a papyrus in Egypt may yet give us Mark's autograph copy and tell us just how the Gospel did end.

CHAPTER VI

STREETER'S THEORY OF LOCAL TEXTS

The most brilliant contribution to the theory of New Testament textual criticism since the epoch-making work of Hort is the new volume by Canon B. H. Streeter, *The Four Gospels* (1925). A new edition with important additions appeared in 1926. Dr. Streeter has carried on the work of Sanday, but he has done a great deal of original study and constructive thinking. There are only 148 pages devoted to the subject of textual criticism besides four valuable appendices, pp. 565 to 597. The rest of the volume, pp. 149 to 562, deals with Synoptic Criticism which is shown to be closely connected with textual criticism. But it is beaten oil and requires close reading and deserves the fullest scrutiny. The importance of the book is shown by the fact that Burkitt devotes pp. 278 to 294 of *The Journal of Theological Studies for April*, 1925, to a careful, sympathetic, enthusiastic, and yet critical estimate of the positions taken by Streeter. The puzzle of Hort about the Western type of text is taken up by Streeter, who proposes to confine the use of the term "Western" to the geographically early Western like k e W^{mk} (Africa) and a b D (Italy-Gaul). The other early "Western" documents, like Syr^{sin} and Syr^{cur} (located in Antioch) he proposes to call Eastern,

STREETER'S THEORY OF LOCAL TEXTS

a new family name on a par with the geographical Western. But Streeter finds another local division of the Eastern text in Cæsarea which he terms fam θ. The letter θ is applied to the newly discovered Koridethi uncial. This manuscript "was discovered in a remote valley in the Caucasus, where it had long been a kind of village fetish; but at a much earlier date it belonged to a monastery at Koridethi — at the far end of the Black Sea just inside the old frontier between Russia and Turkey" (*The Four Gospels*, p. 791). The manuscript probably belongs to the eighth century A.D. It is not early and is not a pure text, but it has been shown by Kirsopp Lake in *The Harvard Theological Review* for July, 1923, to belong to the same family as the famous Ferrar group of cursives (now known to be twelve in all (*Four Gospels*, p. 80), Codex 1 and its allies (fam. 1), Paris Ms 28, 2 pe (81 of Hort), 700. This theory of a Cæsarean text is the most important addition in textual theory that Streeter makes. The differences between early Western documents were already known as between Syr^{sin} and ^{cur} on the one hand and k e a b D on the other. Streeter also proposes to drop Hort's distinction between Neutral and Alexandrian and to call them both simply Alexandrian. Something can be said for this view for "Neutral" seems to beg the question in advance and Alexandrian can be used for both on a stretch. Though Hort's Alexandrian text is certainly a variation from the same stock as the Neutral whatever it is called. Streeter also proposes the name Byzantine for Syrian and that can be done with no loss and Griesbach long ago proposed this name for it.

But it must be confessed that the Cæsarean type of text is not clearly made out. Burkitt says (*Journal of Theol. Studies*, April, 1925, p. 284): "I confess to a sort of prejudice against it, a feeling that the actual facts of the textual tradition are not so easily described in terms of history and geography. In particular I find it rather difficult to split up the non-Byzantine, Non-Alexandrian, non-Western texts into two branches." That statement represents my own reaction to this phase of Streeter's theory of a Cæsarean text. "My chief objection to speaking of 'the Cæsarean text' is that this term gives apparent definiteness and consistence to a set of 'various readings' that remain to me obstinately disparate and amorphous" (Burkitt, *op. cit.*, p. 284). It is plain, therefore, that Streeter's views will be sifted very carefully by scholars before they are adopted as on a par with or in place of those of Hort. Burkitt says (*op. cit.*, p. 288) "that in the vast welter of variants represented by D W lat. afr. eur. on the one hand, and by θ 565, 1 &c., 28, 69–124 &c., 700, with Syr. $^{s.\ et\ c.,}$ on the other, are to be formed a number of true readings and that in some cases these readings occur in places where ℵ and B (and consequently Dr. Hort) have gone wrong. But I do not think we can do more than consider the readings one by one on their merits." That appears a sound conclusion for present day scholarship. Time alone can tell how general may be the use of Streeter's new nomenclature in place of that of Hort which is retained in my *Introduction to the Textual Criticism of the New Testament* (1925). Von Soden's attempt may be pronounced a failure. A better fate will likely come to the work of Streeter. In the *Journal of Theological Studies for July, 1925*, pp. 373 to 378 Streeter makes a careful reply to Burkitt's criticism of the theory of a Cæsarean type of text and Burkitt (pp. 378 to 380) has a final word in defence of his criticism. Here the matter will probably rest till more light is thrown on the subject. Burkitt holds to the essential oneness of the Eastern type of text. "I cannot see any fundamental separation between any of these interesting Eastern texts" (p. 380). But I wish to record my own gratitude to Streeter for his brilliant piece of work.

CHAPTER VII

WHEN THE WESTERN TEXT IS RIGHT

There is no problem connected with the textual criticism of the New Testament more perplexing than the value of the Western type of text. It was not difficult for Hort to show that all purely Syrian readings were wrong. Burgon and Miller argued vigorously in defence of the Syrian type of text as preserved in the *Textus Receptus*, but the verdict among New Testament scholars has gone to Hort by the sheer weight of the facts. A purely Syrian reading with no pre-Syrian witnesses stands convicted of being erroneous. The same line of argument applies to the purely Alexandrian readings. There are no documents that always give Alexandrian readings. Mixture marks all these documents. They show (often) now a Neutral and Alexandrian reading, now and then a Western and Alexandrian reading, occasionally a purely Alexandrian reading, or one supported also by the Syrian class which here followed the Alexandrian class. A reading of the Alexandrian class supported by the Neutral or the Western class has to be decided at bottom on the relative merits of the Neutral and Western classes and by internal evidence. A purely Alexandrian reading is certain to be wrong, a mere scholarly correction to remove a difficulty. The support of the Syrian class in such a reading counts for nothing against the Neutral and Western classes. so far the theory of Westcott and Hort carries conviction with the great majority of modern scholars, certainly in Britain and America. It remains to be seen how far the new method of von Soden will win a hearing in Germany. It has won little favor elsewhere because of its over-refinement and complications.

Westcott and Hort pinned their faith to the superior worth of the Neutral type of text as the nearest approach to the original text of the New Testament now available. They did not claim that in all respects it corresponded with the autograph text. Hort himself pointed out some sixty-five cases where he thought emendation was necessary to restore the original text now lost from all known documents. The name "Neutral" is unfortunate, for it seems to beg the questions in dispute. But the name has been accepted in lieu of a better one.

Objection can also be made to the term Western, which applies to the Old Syriac of the East as truly as to the Old Latin of the West. But names do not carry one very far in a question like this. As a matter of fact about the beginning of the third century A.D. traces of the use of the Western text can be found in all parts of the Christian world of which we possess literary remains. The Western text seems to be dominant. But Hort warns us against thinking that there was no other type of text in existence. Barnard (*Clement of Alexandria's Biblical Text*, 1899) has shown that Clement of Alexandria used the Western type of text, as did Origen after him sometimes. But Origen more frequently employed manuscripts that corresponded to the Neutral or Alexandrian type of text. The wholesale destruction of Christian manuscripts by Imperial persecution, by the Goths and Vandals, by the Saracens, compels one to be cautious about the evidence for the early types of text.

It is now a disputed point whether in point of fact the Western type of text is not older than the Neutral, whether the Neutral is not a revision of the Western. These two points are not necessarily connected. Our oldest uncials only go back to the fourth century A.D., Codex Vaticanus (B) and Codex Sinaiticus (ℵ), but these prevailingly give the Neutral type of text, especially B, save in the Pauline Epistles where even B has Western readings. But there are papyri fragments that go back to the third century, like $\mathfrak{p}^1$ (Matt. 1: 1-9, 12, 14-20) and $\mathfrak{p}^5$ (John 1: 23-31, 33-41; 20: 11-17). These fragments support the Neutral type of text like ℵ and B. But, on the other hand, the Old Syriac and the Old Latin Versions seem to antedate these early documents, and both of these versions support, as a rule, the Western text. But k of the African Latin, fourth or fifth century A.D., follows a Greek text that agrees now with D and now with B. That is to say, the Codex Bobiensis is Neutral nearly as often as it is Western. Besides, the Sinaitic Syriac (syr^{sin}) and the Curetonian Syriac (syr^{cu}) often disagree with each other. Hence it seems clear that the Western text at first was not homogeneous, but more or less local and varied with different strata. The evidence for the Neutral text may not be as old as some forms of the

WHEN THE WESTERN TEXT IS RIGHT 83

Western text, but it represents a more consistent text. With the evidence before us one is disposed to say that the Neutral text is probably a careful revision of an earlier text now lost to us, while the Western is a corruption of that same earlier text.

If follows, therefore, that neither the Neutral nor the Western is always right. Bornemann did argue that the Western is always right and the best text, but he gained no following. Hort is the stoutest defender of the Neutral text, but he does not contend that it is always right. On the other hand, Hort admits that Western non-interpolations are often correct. That is simply another way of saying that there are Neutral interpolations, where the Western text represents the original against some additions in the Neutral text. The number of these is comparatively small in comparison with the additions and corruptions in the Western text. Hort gives the list of the more important or exceptional instances on p. 176 of *The New Testament in Greek*, vol. ii. Some of these additions to the Neutral text Hort considers spurious, as in Matthew 27:49; Luke 22:19*b*, 20; 24:3, 6, 12, 40, 52, 53. And yet Westcott and Hort print these additions in their Greek text, though with double brackets to indicate serious doubt. But why print them at all if they are not genuine? The purpose of Westcott and Hort is not to print the Neutral text, but the true text so far as it is possible to find it. It looks a bit like slavery to B or ℵ B or to the Neutral text to print these readings which Hort holds to be interpolations. He would not print them if they were Western interpolations. It is plain that Hort is very reluctant to admit that the

Western is right against the Neutral, even in these Western non-interpolations.

Most of the instances are small additions in the Neutral text, except in the case of Matthew 27:49, Luke 22:19b, 20; 24:12, 40, where whole sentences are involved. In Matthew 27:49 the spurious addition is derived from John 19:34, where it is a genuine part of the text. It makes nonsense of the text in Matthew 27:49, because v. 50 adds that Jesus spoke in a loud voice and gave up the spirit. That is to say, he died after the piercing of his side by the soldier. This scribal blunder gained such a grip that it appears in Chrysostom and Cyril of Alexandria, besides being in ℵ B C L U T and some of the cursives 5, 48, 67, 115, 127* gat mm (of the Vulgate) syr$^{hr\ semel}$ aeth. This reading of the Neutral (and Alexandrian) class is clearly wrong on both transcriptional and intrinsic grounds. The Western class rejects it, as does the Syrian. Certainly the text of Westcott and Hort should not have this blunder in it. It is true that Von Soden inserts it with brackets, but he follows his own textual theory, not that of Hort. W agrees with the Western documents against the passage. The Old Latin is against it, but the Old Syriac fails us here. Either this passage was omitted by the Western text, or added by the Neutral. Hort (vol. ii., *Notes on Select Readings*, p. 22) seems unable to act decisively: "We have thought it on the whole right to give expression to this view by including the words within double brackets, though we did not feel justified in removing them from the text, and are not prepared to reject altogether the alternative supposition."

WHEN THE WESTERN TEXT IS RIGHT

That lame conclusion seems to be due to undue deference to the Neutral class.

There is more doubt about the true text in Luke 22: 19b, 20, for the documents of the Western class differ very much among themselves. W here goes with the Neutral and Alexandrian classes in having the passage. Some of the Western documents (c f g vg) omit the passage altogether. D a ff² i l omit the passage, but transpose vv. 17, 18. The Old Latin b e do not omit, but transpose vv. 17, 18 to the end of v. 19. Syr^{cu} omits v. 20, but has v. 19b, syr^{sin} has v. 19 and part of v. 20; "after they had supped, he took the cup" and "this is my blood, the new testament," but with v. 17 in between. The order of the verses in syr^{sin} is 16, 19, 20a, 17, 20b, 18–21. The same order appears in syr^{cu}, except that v. 20 does not appear. In b (Codex Veronensis) the order is 16, 19, 17, 16, 21, 22. Those that omit avoid the repetition of the cup. The argument from transcriptional evidence is hard to catch. It might seem to be an effort to reproduce the language of Paul in 1 Corinthians 11: 24, 25. And this was done in successive stages as the variations in the Western manuscripts show. But the repetition of the cup may have led a scribe to omit, as it did some to transpose, the order of the clauses to get rid of the repetition. There were four cups in the observance of the passover, but scribes may have come to refer both cups in Luke to the Supper. Hence one would be dropped. It is a nicely balanced question. Intrinsic evidence gives no decided argument. In the light of the whole evidence it is not clear why Hort felt so certain about it, while so uncertain about Matthew

27:49. He concludes (*op. cit.*, p. 64) that the difficulties "leave no moral doubt that the words in question were absent from the original text of Luke, notwithstanding the purely Western ancestry of the documents which omit them." To me the problem is more complicated here than in Matthew 27:49. Von Soden prints Luke 22:19b, 20 without brackets. The balance of evidence is slightly in favor of the genuineness of this passage, though it is by no means certain.

In Luke 24:12 both W and syr[sin] agree with syr[cu et sch et p] c f ff² vg along with the Neutral, Alexandrian, and Syrian classes in retaining this verse against D a b e l fu. Hort calls this verse "a Western non-interpolation" (*op. cit.*, p. 71). He considers it a condensation of John 20:3–10. But the junction of syr[sin] with syr[cu] makes the passage very early and shows that the omission is purely Western geographically. The problem is not so clear now. The omission has only partial support from the Western documents. Von Soden prints it without brackets.

In Luke 24:40 both syr[cu] and syr[sin] join D a b e ff² l in rejecting the verse, while W goes with the Neutral, Alexandrian, and Syrian classes in retaining it. Here the Western documents include the Old Syriac and some of the Old Latin, including e of the African Latin, a pretty clear case. Besides, the verse seems to be "a natural adaptation" (Hort) from John 20:20. Von Soden brackets this verse.

The other Western non-interpolations with double brackets in Westcott and Hort's Greek New Testament are short clauses or phrases in Luke 24:3, 6, 36, 51, 52. Von Soden prints τοῦ Κυρίου Ἰησοῦ in Luke 24:3, a

WHEN THE WESTERN TEXT IS RIGHT

Western non-interpolation, and the first of a series in this chapter. But only D a b e ff² l Eus omit all three words, geographical Western again, while 42 f sah syr^(cu et sch) have τοῦ Ἰησοῦ without κυρίου. The Western documents are divided, and the question arises whether the name was added or accidentally dropped. The other classes have all three words. The Western class does not seem indubitably right in this omission. Hort objects to it also because the words "the Lord Jesus" do not occur in the Gospels outside of Mark 16: 19.

In Luke 24: 6 the case is not quite so clear as Hort seems to think. He calls it an antithetic form of Mark 16: 6 (= Matt. 28: 6) and a Western non-interpolation. But both syr^(cu), and syr^(sin) have the words: "He is not here, but is risen." Again the Western documents are divided, while W also has it, reading ἀνέστη instead of ἠγέρθη. It is omitted only by D a b e ff² l. One at any rate has proof of a common document for these readings that was used by this group of Western manuscripts in the West. Von Soden prints the words without brackets.

In Luke 24: 36 syr^(sin) and syr^(cu) again combine with W, giving the words: "And he says to them, Peace unto you." W adds before Εἰρήνη the words Ἐγώ εἰμει, μὴ φοβεῖσθαι as do G P 88. 127. 130 ^(Gk et Lat) c f g^(1, 2.) vg etc. The words about "Peace" are rejected by the same group of Western documents D a b e ff² l. Von Soden brackets these words. Hort considers this Neutral interpolation an adaptation from John 20: 19. But the Western documents are again divided, and there are three readings. Clearly the addition in W and the others agreeing with it is from John 6:20. That fact throws doubt also on the other clause as a like addition from John 20:19, where it is undoubtedly genuine.

In Luke 24:51 the same Western group D a b e ff², with the help of ℵ and Aug reject the words καὶ ἀνεφέρετο εἰς τὸν οὐρανόν. The syr^sin here has only the words "he was lifted up from them." All the documents have διέστη ἀπ' αὐτῶν, which practically means the Ascension, which is plainly stated in Acts 1:2, 9–11. Hort is confident the addition is due to the assumption that the separation of Jesus from the disciples meant the Ascension. Von Soden brackets the words. Probably the words were added from Acts, unless, forsooth, they were inadvertently dropped. One feels that the last word has not been said about the agreement of D a b e ff² l in Lk 24.

In Luke 24:52 the syr^sin joins D a b e ff² l and Aug in rejecting προσκυνήσαντες αὐτόν. Von Soden brackets the words. Hort thinks that this addition is a natural sequel to καὶ ἀνεφέρετο εἰς τὸν οὐρανόν in v. 51 by the same documents due to Matthew 28:9, 17. The dodging of syr^{sin et cu} back and forth on these Western non-interpolations is interesting. But clearly Hort has shown that the Western class can be right as against the Neutral. He feels "more doubtful" about the omission of ἀπὸ τοῦ μνημείου (Luke 24:9), though supported by the same documents D a b e ff² l, with the addition of c arm. Hence Hort uses only single brackets here. But the sense seems to call for ἀπὸ τοῦ μνημείου. So one is compelled to wonder what sort of a document explains these interesting readings in Luke 24. Was it the

WHEN THE WESTERN TEXT IS RIGHT

original copy of Luke, or was it a sleepy scribe that fell down in his work in this closing chapter?

The most important remaining Western non-interpolations where Westcott and Hort use only single brackets because not certainly wrong are Matthew 6: 15 τὰ παραπτώματα αὐτῶν; 6: 25 ἢ τί πίητε; 9: 34 οἱ δὲ φαρισαῖοι...δαιμόνια; 13: 33 ἐλάλησεν αὐτοῖς; 21: 44 καὶ ὁ πεσὼν ...λικμήσει αὐτόν; 23: 26 καὶ τῆς παροψίδος; Mark 2: 22 ἀλλὰ οἶνον νέον εἰς ἀσκοὺς καινούς; 10: 2 προσελθόντες φαρισαῖοι; 14: 39 τὸν αὐτὸν λόγον εἰπών; Luke 5: 39 οὐδείς. . . . χρηστός ἐστιν; 10: 41 f. μεριμνᾷς. . . . ἢ ἑνός; 12: 19 κείμενα. . . . φάγε, πίε; 22: 62 καὶ . . . ἔκλαυσεν πικρῶς; John 3: 31 ἐπάνω πάντων ἐστίν; 3: 32 τοῦτο; 4: 9 οὐ γὰρ . . . Σαμαρείταις. If each of these cases be examined in detail, it will be found that the evidence varies in each instance, as we found to be true in those printed by Westcott and Hort with double brackets. Some of them will be acknowledged by almost any scholar to be right, cases where the Western represents the true text and the Neutral an interpolation. But each reading stands or falls on its merits according to the evidence. The problem cannot be handled by a blanket phrase like Western non-interpolations, though it is true that the Western type is more frequently right in such cases than in Western additions. But some Western so-called non-interpolations may be simply Western omissions.

An instance of Western addition that Hort prints with double brackets appears in Luke 22: 43, 44, the passage about the visit of the angel and the sweat-like drops of blood. The Neutral Class (A B R T W 13* syr[sin]) rejects the passage. It is significant that both W and syr[sin] join B here. The manuscript evidence against the genuineness is visibly strengthened. The Western, Alexandrian, and Syrian classes have it, though some of the Greek manuscripts and versions have obelisks or asterisks indicating doubt, and some of the Fathers express doubt about it and note its absence in many early documents. It looks as if this passage stands on a par with the addition in John 5: 4, except that ℵ is against John 5: 4, but supports Luke 22: 43-44. But a corrector of ℵ (ℵ^a) erased it here. Transcriptional evidence is against it. Von Soden brackets it. Hort (*op. cit.*, p. 67) considers it a true incident and a precious remnant of evangelic tradition.

But what shall one say of Luke 23: 34? Here again Westcott and Hort print this precious passage with double brackets. Hort (*op. cit.*, p. 68) says: "We cannot doubt that it comes from an extraneous source." It is, according to Hort, not a part of Luke's Gospel, but he thinks it a genuine saying of Jesus and that "it has exceptional claims to be permanently retained, with the necessary safeguards, in its accustomed place." That strikes one as a curious conclusion for a scholar with positive conviction of its lack of genuineness. The only proper place for it, if not genuine, is in an explanatory footnote. Hort calls it "a Western interpolation of limited range in early times." It is absent from B D W 38. 435. a b d syr^{sin} sah cop^{dz}. The case against it is strengthened by the evidence of W and syr^{sin}, which Hort did not know. But, if B were absent, Hort would call its absence a Western non-interpolation instead of its presence a Western addition. The earliest evidence for it is Western also, as African Latin e and syr^{cu}, both East and West

WHEN THE WESTERN TEXT IS RIGHT

and hence not of "limited range." B here deserts its usual company, ℵ A C L Δ, and one wonders if it really represents the Neutral reading or a sporadic Western omission, though W reinforces B and is sometimes Neutral. It does not appear that the evidence against Luke 23: 34 is quite so positive as Hort seems to think. Von Soden does not bracket it. Hort is open sometimes to the charge of standing by B, right or wrong. No single document, not even B, is always right. A similar difficulty arises in Luke 15: 21 about the addition of ποίησόν με ὡς ἕνα τῶν μισθίων σου, which is rejected by ℵ B D U X al [20] gat mm cat[ox] [119]. The Old Syriac is wanting here, but the Old Latin has it and W also. Here again D appears in company with B (and ℵ) and away from the other Western documents. Transcriptional evidence is for its omission because of appearance in v. 19, but it is a nicely balanced point, though the balance of evidence is against it. Westcott and Hort print it with single brackets. Von Soden rejects it outright. If B did not have it, Hort would not hesitate a moment in rejecting it. Intrinsic evidence rather opposes it as a finer trait for the son to be interrupted before he finishes his speech.

It is clear, then, without attempting to examine all of the distinctive Western readings, that the Western class is sometimes right as against the Neutral class. It is probably more frequently right than Hort admitted or knew. Turner (*The Study of the New Testament*, 1920, p. 58) is sure that the Western text has something to contribute toward the reconstruction of the original text of the New Testament and that its contribution must be weighed on its merit, not merely on its age. Souter ("Progress in Textual Criticism of the Gospels since Westcott and Hort," in *Mansfield College Essays*, 1909, p. 363) thinks that "the combination of syr^{sin} and k would now generally be regarded as sufficient to upset the combination B ℵ, or, in other words, the version may sometimes have retained the correct text, where all known Greek MSS. have lost it." He thinks, however, that the alteration of the text of Westcott and Hort would be small if they had known the new manuscripts now accessible to us. In particular, when the Old Syriac combines with the Old Latin, a strong presumptive case is made out. Valentine Richards (*Cambridge Biblical Essays*, p. 534) thinks that "a further discimination of the different types of Western, or rather of second century, text is one of the most pressing needs of the present day." It is a great advance to see that. A reading can no longer be condemned because it is Western. But we must not go to the other extreme. The Western documents differ widely and radically in many readings. The simple truth is that we are not yet in a position to lay down a definite procedure for deciding the merits of Western readings. There is here a rich field for study and research. It will have to be attacked in detail and as a whole. A fresh study of the whole problem is called for by competent scholars.

Only a word can be given to the special Western readings in Acts. These are mainly additions and are very numerous. Blass proposed the theory of two editions of both Gospel and Acts by Luke, to explain the Western non-interpolations in the Gospel and the Western additions in the Acts. But his

WHEN THE WESTERN TEXT IS RIGHT

theory has not won a strong following. The text of Acts is still a matter of debate. Ramsay, Harnack, Chase, Rendel Harris, Burkitt, Ropes, and others have contributed their quota to the discussion. In general, it may be said that the Western additions in Acts do not stand in as favorable a light as the Western non-interpolations in the Gospel of Luke.

CHAPTER VIII

SOME INTERESTING READINGS IN THE WASHINGTON CODEX OF THE GOSPELS

In 1912 Professor Alexander Souter wrote in his excellent handbook, *The Text and Canon of the New Testament* (p. 31), concerning the newly discovered "Freer Gospels," bought in Egypt by Mr. C. L. Freer of Detroit and now in Washington (hence called W by Gregory): "to this MS. one can merely call attention, as at the moment of writing very little is known about it." But in that same year Professor H. A. Sanders, of the University of Michigan, published a *Facsimile of the Washington MS. of the Four Gospels in the Freer Collection* (pp. x. 372), and issued at the same time *The Washington MS. of the Four Gospels* (pp. vii. 247), an elaborate discussion and collation of W. He has presented the essential facts, so far as known, concerning the history of the document. It belongs either to the fourth or to the fifth century, as is plain from the style, uncial writing, infrequent punctuation, absence of accents and of the Eusebian sections, etc. The Gospels appear in the Western order like that in D and the Old Latin (a, b, e, f, ff²), *i.e.*, Matthew, John, Luke, Mark. But Sanders devotes most of the space in the latter volume to a discussion of the problem of the text, arguing against the textual theory of Westcott and Hort and in favor of Von Soden's text. "A comparison of the readings of W with Von Soden's results, as shown in his prolegomena, convinced me that Tischendorf and Westcott and Hort had built on a false foundation" (p. 41). Now there is no connection at all between the theory of Tischendorf and that of Westcott and Hort. But Sanders definitely takes Hoskier's side in his attack (*Codex B and its Allies*, 1914) on Westcott and Hort. He has accepted the classification of documents given by Von Soden, so that his exposition of the critical data found in W is vitiated for most modern students.

Professor E. J. Goodspeed, of the University of Chicago, is a disciple of Westcott and Hort. He published in 1914 *The Freer Gospels*, in which he carefully collates all the important readings. "It will be understood that our basis of collation is the full, continuous text of Westcott-Hort" (p. 7). He has a few pertinent remarks in closing. "In type of text W is curiously heterogeneous, showing three somewhat distinct strata, Neutral, Western, Syrian. Matthew and Luke 8–24 are decidedly Syrian in type. John and Mark 1–7 are Neutral, with some interesting Western readings interspersed, *e.g.*, the omission of the Lucan genealogy. The primitive subscription κατα Ιωαννην is a further hint of the Neutral ancestry of this part of the MS. Mark is decidedly Western throughout, and while its readings are often not those of D they are usually of the same general kind as they, and so illustrate Hort's feeling that the Western is as much a textual tendency as a definite textual type" (p. 64). The temper of this comment suits me far better than the interpretation of Professor Sanders. I do not maintain that Hort said the last word in textual criticism, but nothing has yet been brought to light that shows he was on the wrong tack. There is need of a full, fresh study of W by an adherent of Hort.

One has in W a text of the Gospels copied by a fourth or fifth century scribe, and corrected by himself and three later hands. But in spite of these efforts to remove errors, many remain, like the repetition of John vi. 54b, 56a after πίνων μου τὸ αἷμα in verse 56, a clear case of homoioteleuton. It seems clear that the scribe of W did not copy one single manuscript, however. This codex is a splendid illustration of mixture, as Hort expounded it. The scribe either had access to a number of documents with different ancestries, or the manuscript (if only one) used by him had a diverse ancestry.

For myself I am prepared to argue that W shows Alexandrian readings as well as Neutral, Western, and Syrian. Thus in Matthew 1:25 the Neutral class (א B 2, 33) with some Western support (a[vid] b c g[1] k sah cop syr[sin] syr[cur] Amb) reads υἱόν, while the Alexandrian (CLΔW) and Syrian (EKMS al pler syr[utr] Egypt) with some Western support (D f ff[1] g[2] arm Eth Aug) read τὸν υἱὸν αὐτῆς τὸν πρωτότοκον. In this instance, to be sure, W may be Syrian instead of Alexandrian, but the Alexandrian class is here.

In Matthew 5:22, εἰκῆ is properly rejected again by the Neutral class (א B vg Or) and added by the Western, Alexandrian (LΔW cop), and Syrian, including syr[sin] (Western) and W. In Matthew 6:1 the Neutral (א B

1, 209, al Or) and Western (D it vg Hil. Aug. Hier.) classes read rightly δικαιοσύνην, while the Alexandrian (WLΔ) and Syrian (EKMSUZ al pler syr^p go arm al Chrys) read ἐλεημοσύνην with f, k of the Old Latin, and א^a syr^{cur} have the colorless δόσιν. In Matthew 6:4 and 6 ἐν τῷ φανερῷ is rightly rejected by the Western and Neutral classes, while it is added by the Alexandrian (WLΔ) and Syrian. The doxology in Matthew 6:13 is rejected by the Neutral (אB 1, 17, 118, 130, 209 cop Or) and Western (D a b c ff^{1}g^2 l vg Cyp Tert), but appears in the Alexandrian (WLΔ) and Syrian (late documents), with some Western support, though k syr^{cur} and sah all have different shorter forms of it. In Matthew 9:13, again, W joins the Neutral (אBWΔ 1, 22, 33, 118, 209, syr^{utr}) and Western (D most Old Latin, vg arm Eth Aug) against the addition of εἰς μετάνοιαν, which is inserted from Luke 5:32 by the Alexandrian (CL sah cop) and Syrian classes. In Matthew 14:15 W goes with the Neutral, Western and Syrian classes against the addition of οὖν by the Alexandrian (א CZ cop Or). Classification is difficult at Matthew 19:16, for σχῶ is read by Neutral documents like BC, ἔχω by Alexandrian (WΔ) and Syrian, while א L 28, 33, 77, 157, 238, syr^{cur} cop have κληρονομήσω, which seems Western in spite of the absence of D (with B). In Matthew 21:44 W accompanies the Western class in omitting the addition. In Matthew 24:36 the Neutral and Western classes have οὐδὲ ὁ υἱός, as in Mark 13:32, while the Alexandrian (WLΔ cop) and Syrian reject it with syr^{sin}. In Matthew 27:49 W goes with the Western and Syrian classes in rejecting properly the addition from

John 19:34, though this obvious insertion is supported by the Neutral class. One pauses here for a moment to wonder if the Alexandrian class is represented by CL with the Neutral or by WΔ cop Or with the Western and Syrian. It is one of Hort's Western non-interpolations (in other words Neutral interpolations).

In John 1:18, W reads υἱός, not θεός, agreeing with the Western and Syrian classes against the Neutral and Alexandrian. In John 5:1 W follows the Neutral and Western in reading ἑορτὴ τῶν Ἰουδαίων against the Alexandrian ἡ ἑορτὴ τῶν Ἰουδαίων, while in 4:44 it gives τῶν Ἰουδαίων instead of the Western and Syrian τῆς Γαλιλαίας or the Neutral and Alexandrian τῆς Ἰουδαίας, an evident effort to evade the question whether "Judæa" included Galilee. In John 5:3 W agrees with the Western and Syrian classes in reading ἐκδεχομένων τὴν τοῦ ὕδατος κίνησιν. In 5:4 it is with the Neutral and Western in rejecting the whole verse about the periodic visit of the angel to the pool, which is inserted by the Alexandrian and Syrian classes, with some early Western documents (e of the African Latin). In 7:8 W reads οὔπω with the Neutral, Alexandrian (BLWTΔ f g q sah), and Syrian (ΓΛ, al pler syr^{sch et p}), against the Western οὐκ. But it is more probable that the Western here is right. W joins the Neutral and Alexandrian classes in rejecting the Pericope Adulteræ (John 7:53–8:11), and in 13:2 it sides with the Neutral in reading γινομένου instead of γενομένου. In John 16:24, instead of ἵνα πεπληρωμένη, W has the curious reading ἵνα πεπληρωμένη ἦν. This use of ἦν may be a mere lapse of the scribe or it may represent the irrational ν which is so common in the papyri, in which case it would be meant for a subjunctive after all.

In Luke 2:14 W lines up with the Neutral and Western classes for εὐδοκίας, against the Alexandrian and Syrian correction εὐδοκία. As we have said, the genealogy of 3:23-39 is absent from W. In 5:26 W goes with the Western class in omitting the first half of the verse, while in 6:1 it sides with the Neutral and Alexandrian in rejecting the unintelligible δευτεροπρώτῳ which is supported by the Western and Syrian. In Luke 8:43 W agrees with B in inserting ἰατροῖς προσαναλώσασα ὅλον τὸν βίον (cf. Mark 5:26), and in 10:42 it reads ἑνὸς δέ ἐστιν χρεία with the Western, Alexandrian, and Syrian classes against the Neutral (conflate) ὀλίγων δέ ἐστιν χρεία ἢ ἑνός (38 arm syr^hkl read ὀλίγων δέ ἐστιν χρεία). As often, the Western documents are divided here. In 15:21 W omits ποίησόν με ὡς ἕνα τῶν μισθίων σου, with the Western, Alexandrian, and Syrian, against the neutral interpolation; in 15:24 W seems to stand alone, however, in omitting ἦν ἀπολωλὸς καὶ εὑρέθη. In Luke 23:34 W joins B Δ 38, 435, a b d cop syr^sin in omitting the beautiful saying. Is this the combination of the Neutral text and the Western? If so, the verse will have to go. But there is strong Western testimony (African Latin e and syr^cur besides c f ff² L vg) besides the Alexandrian and Syrian. And what if B itself is Western here? In Luke 23:45 W goes with the Western and the Syrian classes in reading καὶ ἐσκοτίσθη ὁ ἥλιος instead of τοῦ ἡλίου ἐκλιπόντος (Neutral and Alexandrian), and in 24:53 it follows the Syrian in reading αἰνοῦντες καὶ εὐλογοῦντες, the conflate reading which combines the Neutral and Alexandrian εὐλογοῦντες and the Western αἰνοῦντες.

In Mark 1:1 W has υἱοῦ θεοῦ with the Neutral, Western, and Syrian classes; in 1:2 it reads ἐν τοῖς προφήταις with the Syrian against the pre-Syrian ἐν τῷ Ἡσαΐᾳ τῷ προφήτῃ. In 1:3 W along with the Old Latin inserts what is in Luke 3:5, 6 and Isaiah 40:4, 5. In Mark there are also frequent minor omissions and frequent transpositions (as in all the Gospels). In 7:4 W reads βαπτίοωνται with the Western and Syrian texts against the Alexandrian (LΔ) βαπτίζωνται and the Neutral ραντίσωνται. In 13:2 W goes with the Western class in adding καὶ διὰ τριῶν ἡμερῶν ἄλλος ἀναστήσεται ἄνευ χειρῶν. But the distinctive addition in Mark is at the end of 16:14, where W, giving the long ending (so Western, Alexandrian, and Syrian), presents this strange apocryphal addition which had been only indirectly known before:

κἀκεῖνοι ἀπελογοῦντε λέγοντες ὅτι ὁ αἰὼν οὗτος τῆς ἀνομίας καὶ τῆς ἀπιστίας ὑπὸ τὸν σατανᾶν ἐστιν ὁ μὴ ἐῶν τὰ ὑπὸ τῶν πνευμάτων ἀκάθαρτα τὴν ἀλήθειαν τοῦ θεοῦ καταλαβέσθαι δύναμιν. διὰ τοῦτο ἀποκάλυψόν σου τὴν δικαιοσύνην ἤδη· ἐκεῖνοι ἔλεγον τῷ Χριστῷ. καὶ ὁ Χριστὸς ἐκείνοις προσέλεγεν ὅτι πεπλήρωται ὁ ὅρος τῶν ἐτῶν τῆς ἐξουσίας τοῦ σατανᾶ ἀλλὰ ἐγγίζει δινὰ καὶ ὑπὲρ ὧν ἐγὼ ἁμαρτησάντων παρεδόθην εἰς θάνατον ἵνα ὑποστρέψωσιν εἰς τὴν ἀλήθειαν καὶ μηκέτι ἁμαρτήσωσιν· ἵνα τὴν ἐν τῷ οὐρανῷ πνευματικὴν καὶ ἄφθαρτον τῆς δικαιοσύνης δόξαν κληρονομήσωσιν.

It is certain that this addition was no part of the long ending of Mark as probably written by Ariston (the Aristion of Papias) to complete the Gospel.

From this rapid survey of some important readings in

W it is plain that mixture is its chief characteristic. Early as it undoubtedly is, it does not rank with ℵ or B. It is more like A in its mixed character. But it will repay careful study precisely because of the complex character of the text which it contains. We can no longer condemn a reading because it is Western. The Western class has various strata in it, and is anything but homogeneous. If the Neutral class is a revision, the Western has a conglomeration of readings in the various documents that preserve it.

CHAPTER IX

PAUL AND HIS BOOKS

Deissmann in his *St. Paul* denies that Paul was a man of literary tastes. He holds that he was a man without the culture of the schools, and that he was in no sense a university man. He compares him to Amos the prophet, who was a herdsman, because he was a tentmaker by trade like Aquila and worked with him in the trade at Corinth (Acts 18: 3). He takes this statement to be proof that Paul belonged distinctly to the artisan class. Besides, Paul frequently speaks of working with his hands at his trade, as in Acts 20: 34; 2 Corinthians 11: 9; 1 Thessalonians 2: 9.

There is no disputing the fact of Paul's self-support by means of his trade, but it does not follow that he was in no sense a man of the schools. It was the Jewish custom for the boy, whatever his calling in life, to know a trade, so that he could do manual labor and be independent and make his own living. It must be confessed that it is a fine custom, and the more's the pity that it is not true of our boys today. In Germany that is the rule, and it was so even for princes of the blood.

But we know expressly that Paul was a student in the school of Gamaliel (Acts 22: 3) in Jerusalem, one of the two rabbinical theological seminaries of the period. Gamaliel was a grandson of Hillel, the founder of the more liberal of the Pharisaic schools, as opposed to that of his rival Shammai. Not only did Paul attend this institution of learning, but he was a diligent student, according to his own claim (Gal. 1:14), and surpassed those of his own age. He was an outstanding student of Judaism, a star pupil of Gamaliel, and probably his hope for the future of his school.

Sir W. M. Ramsay thinks that Paul had come under the influence of the University of Tarsus, his home city, with its great teachers of philosophy. This idea is not accepted by Principal A. E. Garvie of London, who fails to find marks of Hellenic culture in Paul. One may not be able to prove that Paul had a degree from the University of Tarsus, though it is entirely possible in itself. But it is hardly within bounds to affirm that Paul was unresponsive to the intellectual life of his time. He bore himself as well in Athens as in Corinth, and he has many points of contact with the literature of his day. His knowledge of Stoic phrases is so marked that it is actually asserted by some that Paul borrowed from Seneca. He employs the current terms of the mystery-cults, like Gnosticism and Mithraism, to such an extent that it is even claimed that he borrowed from these cults his ruling ideas in theology. He was such a student of Judaism and had such a knowledge of the Old Testament and of Pharisaism, that he is accused of rabbinizing Christianity in spite of his hostility to the Judaizers. Dr. J. Rendel Harris is persuaded that Paul knew not merely two or three of the current Greek poets whom he incidentally quotes, like Epimenides and Menander and others (Acts 17:28; Titus 1:12), but was also familiar with Pindar, Aristophanes, Euripides, and other great Greek writers. Sir W. M. Ramsay considers Paul the greatest philosopher of all time in his powerful grasp of the great problems of life and in his Christocentric conception of the universe.

Certainly, therefore, it is not beside the mark to talk of Paul's intellectual life and habits. His own epistles, ephemeral and personal as some of them may seem to be, yet have the touch of genius in them. He has the quality of illuminating common things and ordinary persons with the glow of reality and the glory of manhood in Christ Jesus. There is no better illustration of this than the Epistle to Philemon, where in one short page he handles the most delicate and difficult questions of personal relationship in a way to give no offence. He at the same time weighs in due proportion the conflicting issues of capital and labor, of autocracy and liberty. Paul shows passion at times that overrides mere rules of grammar, but he sings like a lark in 1 Corinthians 13, and argues like the trained debater in Romans 8 and 1 Corinthians 15.

Paul does not boast of his intellectual attainments, nor brag of the books that he has read, but he denies to his opponents that he is an ignoramus. He claims equality with any of the apostles. "But though I be rude in speech, yet am I not in knowledge" (2 Cor. 11:6). It is easy enough to draw a man's stature wrongly in the ridicule of his ignorant contemporaries. The Stoic and Epicurean philosophers in Athens scouted Paul as a mere babbler or collector of scraps of wisdom

PAUL AND HIS BOOKS

from the Agora, like the sparrow in the street. But these conceited sophists actually thought that Paul was introducing two new gods because he spoke of Jesus and the resurrection. His discourse about Christ and the cross was foolishness to them as to the sophisticated and superficial Corinthians, but Paul himself knew that he was proclaiming the wisdom of God that rose sheer above the shallow and passing theories of men (1 Cor. 2:6).

But Paul took an interest in the intellectual life of others. He wrote to Timothy, "Keep your mind on the reading" (1 Tim. 4:13). This is precisely what the Greek idiom here means. That is the problem with every modern preacher. How can he find time for his books and his study? The good is constantly the enemy of the best. The pastoral work has to be done. There are the sick and the dying, the poor and the needy, the young with their temptations, the old with their sorrows. There are sermons to be made, clubs to attend, committees to meet, one's own health to care for with golf or the motor ride. There are dinners and other functions, and public addresses to deliver, and conventions to which to go. There are the magazines and the papers to keep one up with current events and ideas. One must know his own time, and what men are thinking about now. There is little time left for solid and serious reading. Theological books have lost their flavor. The great poets no longer lure one to the joys of imagination. Historical books are tedious to one who is making history. Scientific books are to be railed at, not to be read, by the modern preacher who finds it much easier to denounce than to understand new discoveries in science or in paleontology.

Where does the Bible come into this maelstrom of the practical preacher's life? Sooth to say, with many it does not come in at all, save as a place from which to get texts to serve as a springboard for one's weekly dive into the deeps of social problems. It was said of one preacher that in his sermons he could go down deeper, and stay down longer, and come up drier than any preacher ever known. The late Sir W. Robertson Nicoll once wrote in *The British Weekly* an editorial on "Books That We Think We Have Read." He mentioned many, but the Bible was the chief one. Many people imagine that they know the Bible better than any other book. As a rule people know very little about it, save a few select passages. And this is true of preachers also who have no habits of study for the Bible or for any books of value. The preacher who does not read will dry up. His sermons will be dull and uninspiring. He will soon change his pastorate, because the barrel will be empty.

But Paul gives us one glimpse into his own hunger for his books. He was the busiest preacher who ever lived. He was missionary and pioneer in planting the gospel where other men had not preached. He was the apostle of the Gentiles, and had a broad statesmanlike grasp of the problem of evangelizing the Roman Empire in his own lifetime. He had theological conflicts with the Judaizers on the one side, and the Gnostics on the other. He had to save Christianity from being a mere ceremonial adjunct to Pharisaism. He had to conserve the heart of the gospel from the vaporings of superficial philosophizing. He had the care of all the churches on his heart, with misunderstandings, bickerings, and jealousies. He had enemies within and without the fold. He lost much precious time in prison. He was persecuted, and had his work rudely interrupted time and again. There was never a preacher who could so little call his time his own. He had long journeys on land and on sea. He met perils of rivers and perils of robbers. He did not shirk the pastoral side of his work. At Ephesus he preached Christ from house to house, as well as on the sabbaths in the schoolhouse of Tyrannus. He had to write letters to individuals and to churches to keep things going. He carried on a great campaign for funds for the poor souls in Jerusalem. He enlisted the coöperation of a multitude of workers. He cultivated the personal touch, and trained a group of gifted young preachers to carry on the work when he was gone. He had to interpret the gospel for men of light and leading who could pass on the torch. He had to put his gospel so that the untaught could understand it. He had to fuse into one the conflicting interests of Jew and Gentile, and mould them into one man in Christ Jesus. He was writing the greatest letters of all time without being a professional letter writer, a sort of spiritual and intellectual by-play. He was and is the greatest interpreter of Christ that the world has ever seen.

But this greatest preacher and pastor and theologian and man of affairs did not neglect his intellectual life.

If one desires the proof of this statement, let him think over the message to Timothy to bring "the book-wrap," as the word translated "cloak" probably means, "and the books, especially the parchments" (2 Tim. 4: 13).

The old preacher is now a prisoner again in Rome. He is facing certain death this time. He misses his friends, who no longer come as before for fear of death themselves. It is now a crime to be a Christian in Rome, since Nero has laid upon them the charge of setting fire to Rome to escape the calumny which he has incurred by his insane crime. Paul had left his bunch of books at the home of Carpus in Troas the last time that he was in the east before going to Macedonia (1 Tim. 1: 3), and to Nicopolis (Tit. 3: 12), where he was probably arrested and brought to Rome. Probably the bundle was larger than Paul could carry conveniently in his travels. He may have expected to come back by Troas soon, but it had turned out otherwise. He misses these books. There is one blessing about books as compared with friends. They are never afraid to be with you, or ashamed of you. There is a special link with old books that one has used and has marked. One knows where to turn for a passage that one loves. The very page stands out before one's eyes.

Paul speaks of two kinds of books, "the books, especially the parchments." The ancients had two kinds of books, the papyrus rolls and the parchment rolls. Later the parchment codex came into use, a book with leather leaves that were used upon both sides of the leaf and bound together. But these came into general use much later, mainly in the fourth century A.D. At first both the papyrus book and the

PAUL AND HIS BOOKS 109

parchment book would be made into a roll. Sometimes the parchment leaves would not be pasted together into a roll, but left in loose form. This may have been the case with the parchments that Paul had left with Carpus. The papyrus rolls were pieces of papyrus glued together, of any convenient length. The columns of writing would be unrolled as one read, while the part just read would be rolled up again. Sometimes the roll would be fastened to a stick at each end. There would often be a case for the roll. The book-wrap would hold a number of these rolls, whether of papyrus or parchment. The leaves of parchment, if not bound together into a codex, would lie open in the book-wrap.

But what were the books that Paul missed and longed to have with him? How much light the contents of that book-wrap would throw upon Paul's mental habits and intellectual tastes! It is possible that there were some notes of his own studies, and addresses such as Luke may have had for Paul's speeches and sermons given in Acts. It is practically certain that there were portions of the Old Testament, probably the parchments, either in Hebrew or in Greek (the Septuagint). He may have made notes on the margin, especially where he found Messianic prophecies. Who would not pay a great price for these old books with Paul's own notes upon them? It has been my good fortune to fall heir to some of the books used by my great teacher and predecessor, John A. Broadus. Whenever I find a passage with notes in his familiar handwriting, there is always peculiar interest and emphasis. My wife has a copy of her father's Greek

New Testament with his notes, which she prizes very greatly.

One can but hope that Timothy brought the books in time for Paul to use them again before the end came. It is not certain that Timothy realized how great a man Paul really was. If he had the faintest conception of the stature of the man who was his spiritual father, he certainly took the best care of these books till he was able to place them in Paul's hands once more. Dr. Stalker has a delightful sermon for children on "Paul's Cloak, Books, and Parchments."

Paul asked Timothy to pick up John Mark and bring him along with him, for he had found him useful for ministry. There is a touch of pathos in this, for Paul had once refused to let Mark go with him again because he had flickered in the crisis at Perga. Paul stoutly resisted the plea of Barnabas to take Mark along the second time. No doubt Mark deserved this severe treatment at the hands of Paul, though one rejoices that Barnabas gave him his second chance. And he had made good. When Paul wrote to the Colossians (4:10) from Rome, he warmly commended John Mark to them in case he came that way. He was then in Rome with Paul, after his experiences with Barnabas and with Peter. It is entirely possible, even likely, that Mark had written his Gospel by the time Paul wrote to the Colossians, and that Paul had read this Gospel and refers to it when he says that Mark had been useful to him for ministry (2 Tim 4:11). There is, of course, no way to prove this interpretation, but Paul had something definite in mind in the compliment bestowed on John Mark. So then it is quite possible that one of the books, perhaps one of the parchment books, was the Gospel of Mark.

It is also possible that both of Luke's books, the Gospel and the Acts, were in that book-wrap. Luke himself was with Paul in Rome. "Luke alone is with me" (2 Tim. 4: 11), loyal to the last to his great and beloved friend. This friendship between Luke and Paul is one of the great friendships of history. And Paul's copies of Luke's books, presentation copies, we might say, may have been in the bunch of books in Troas.

It has been suggested that Paul had left there also copies of his own epistles. That I very much doubt. It is much more likely that he had left there Greek and Latin manuscripts of favorite authors, poets and historians and orators. "As some of your own poets have said" (Acts 17: 28), Paul said to the Athenians, "One of them, a prophet (poet) of their own, said" (Tit. 1: 12), he wrote of the Cretans.

If Dr. J. Rendel Harris makes good his claim about Paul's acquaintance with Aristophanes, Euripides, and Pindar, we shall be compelled to think of Paul as one in touch with the currents of the intellectual life of his times. He was a man of books. He loved books, the best books, his own books. He hungered for the companionship of books. This old preacher turned back to the fellowship of his well-worn books that had stimulated his mind and heart. He yearned most of all for the Scriptures in that book-wrap. They had been the comfort and strength of his ministry. He will want them near him as he faces death and goes to get his crown from the hands of Christ.

Dr. T. H. Darlow has shown in his *Life and Letters of Sir W. Robertson Nicoll* that he had some thirty thousand volumes in his library at Hampstead, books that he had read, some of them many times over, books with his marks and notes written all over them. Nicoll was the foremost bookman of Britain and lived with his books to the end. The prodigious influence that he exerted was in part due to his mastery of books. Paul was a bookman and a man of affairs who knew how to use his books as tools in his workshop.

CHAPTER X

EARLY ENGLISH BIBLES

It is one of the heroic struggles of our race that finally gave men the Bible in the English vernacular so that the people could read it for themselves. It was the sixth century before the gospel gained much power over the people of England though it had been preached there since the second century. Ireland had become strongly Christian. But few people in England could read and there were few copies of the Bible for them to read. These few were Latin manuscripts, the Old Latin Versions, not the Vulgate. Paterson Smyth takes Irish pride in the fact that England owes her earliest Scriptures to the noble libraries of Durrow and Armagh, "when St. Colomb carried his manuscripts to lonely Iona in the days of the glory of the Irish Church, when Ireland was the light of the Western World, and Irishmen went forth from the 'Island of Saints' to evangelize the heathen English" (*How We Got Our Bible*, p. 43).

In the Anglo-Saxon

The travelling preachers in England carried their Latin manuscripts with them and interpreted the Latin Bible to their hearers. The people of Briton spoke many tongues, but finally there was a demand for the Scriptures in Anglo-Saxon. The poet Cædmon, a monk of Whitby, made an alliterative paraphrase of Genesis, Exodus, Daniel about A.D. 670. He paved the way for real translation. Aldhelm, Bishop of Sherborne (died 709), was, so far as known, the first translator of the Psalms into Anglo-Saxon. He is said to have requested Egbert, Bishop of Holy Island, to make a translation of the Gospels into Anglo-Saxon, a copy of which is now in the British Museum. But the Venerable Bede (674 to 735), the monk of Jarrow, "is the head of the long procession of translators of the Bible, stretching from the eighth to the twentieth century" (Price, *The Ancestry of Our English Bible*, p. 210). We know that he himself translated the Gospel of John into Anglo-Saxon, though no part of it has been preserved. Cuthbert tells the pathetic story of the struggle of Bede with death as he was dictating his translation from the Latin. He ran a race with death and won by the narrowest margin. "There remains but one chapter, dear Master, but it seems hard for you to speak," the scribe said. "Nay, it is easy, take thy pen and write quickly," Bede replied. As night drew on, the sobbing scribe whispered: "Master, there is just one sentence more." "Write quickly," he answered. "See, dear Master, it is finished." "Ay, it is finished," Bede replied, as he passed over with the Gloria on his lips. Alfred the Great (848–901) prefaced his code of Saxon laws with a free translation of Exodus 20–23 and the letter sent to the Gentiles in Acts 15. Alfred was engaged in a translation of the Psalms, but did not live to finish it. This enlightened ruler was eager for his people to have the Scriptures in their own tongue. About 950 Alfred made an interlinear gloss on the Latin Landisfarne Gospels and about 990 Ælfric, Archbishop of Canterbury, translated into Anglo-Saxon the Pentateuch, Joshua, Judges, Esther, Job, a part of Kings, and Judith and Maccabees. About 1000 he made a translation of the Gospels with no accompanying Latin text, the earliest preserved to us. One manuscript of Ælfric's work is in Oxford and one in the British Museum. There would be more remains of Anglo-Saxon Scriptures but for the Norman Conquest in 1066. Anglo-Saxon was driven out of court, bar, school, and books. There is no evidence that the whole Bible was ever put into Anglo-Saxon or even all of the New Testament. For three hundred years Anglo-Saxon was taboo in legal, literary, and ecclesiastical circles, but in the end of the day the English tongue won over the French though not without a powerful Norman influence on the language. The outcome is our English language.

Wycliffe's Version

The age of Wycliffe was the age of Chaucer. John Wycliffe (1320–1384) chose to use the English instead of the Latin or the Norman French. He had good company in William Langland, who wrote Piers the Plowman in the English vernacular, and Chaucer's poems followed the same line. William of Shoreham in the first part of the fourteenth century and Richard Rolle by the middle each made a translation of the Psalms into English. Wycliffe was educated at Oxford and was Master of Balliol College for a while.

He resented the oppression of the papacy and found consolation in the study of the Bible. By 1378 he made a plea for an English translation of the Bible and by 1380 he was actively at work on the New Testament while Nicholas of Hereford worked on the Old Testament. Both used the Latin Vulgate. Hereford's work was rudely interrupted in the middle of the verse at Baruch 3:20 and he was brought to trial at Canterbury and excommunicated. Wycliffe had a stroke of paralysis, but went on with his work and either finished the Old Testament or had it done. So the work was finished in 1382. Wycliffe's Bible had a large circulation in spite of being in manuscript. People would pay a load of hay for the privilege of reading it an hour a day. Wycliffe's Lollard preachers carried it far and wide. It looked for a while as if this "morningstar of the Reformation" would bring on the full day that came two centuries later under Martin Luther. But persecution crushed out the Lollards, though a hundred and seventy of the Wycliffe Bibles still exist. Wycliffe turned the tide also in favor of Norman-English as opposed to Norman-French. He was stricken with paralysis again in 1384 and died on the last day of the year at Lutterworth. John Pirvey, a faithful disciple of Wycliffe, revised the whole with much care (1388), but he lamented that the text of the Latin Vulgate was so bad. It needed editing, more than the English, he held. Thus came the completion of the first English Bible. Wycliffe had been excommunicated because of his hatred of ecclesiastical tyranny. He was later denounced by the Archbishop of Canterbury and the High Chancellor of England (Arundel) as "that

EARLY ENGLISH BIBLES

pestilent wretch of damnable memory, son of the old sea serpent, yea the forerunner and disciple of antichrist, who, as the complement of his wickedness, invented a new translation of the Scriptures into his mother tongue" (quoted by Schaff, *Companion to the Greek Testament and English Version*, p. 289). One of the monks called Wycliffe "the organ of the devil, the enemy of the Church, the idol of heretics, the image of hypocrites, the restorer of schism, the storehouse of lies, the sink of flattery," and said that his death was the judgment of God upon him. The Catholic ecclesiastics were violently opposed to the vernacular translation of the Bible into English. The Council of Constance in 1415 not only burned John Hus and Jerome of Prague, but also condemned the writings and the bones of Wycliffe to the flames. So in 1428 his bones were dug up, burned, and cast into the Swift. The Swift, says Fuller, "conveyed them into the Avon, Avon into Severn, Severn into the narrow seas, they into the main ocean; and thus the ashes of Wycliffe are the emblem of his doctrine, which now is dispersed all the world over."

Preparing for William Tindale

The ecclesiastics were bent on keeping the Bible in the vernacular away from the people, but God moves in a mysterious way his wonders to perform. In the fifteenth century the Turks captured Constantinople (1453) and sent Greek scholars in turn to the West. The Renaissance was the outcome with a revival of knowledge of the Greek New Testament in the West when "Greece rose from the grave with the

New Testament in her hand." In 1454 Johann Gutenberg invented movable type for printing. In 1455 the first book from the press was the Latin Vulgate, the Mazarin Bible. In 1458 Greek was taught in the University of Paris. The first Greek grammar was published in 1476. The first Greek lexicon came in 1480. Grocyn in 1492 was the first professor of Greek in Oxford University. Erasmus published the first Greek New Testament in 1516, though Cardinal Ximenes had printed his in 1514. In 1492 Columbus discovered America. On October 31, 1517 Luther nailed his ninety-five theses against the sale of indulgences on the church door at Wittenberg. By the year 1522 translations of the Bible had been printed in most of the languages of Europe, Luther's German Bible appearing that year. But no one had printed an English Bible, though Caxton introduced the printing press into England in 1470.

The Work of Tindale

William Tindale was born in 1484, one year after Luther's birth, and a hundred after the death of Wycliffe. He was born in Gloucestershire near Wales, but was brought up from a child in the University of Oxford and, Foxe says, was "singularly addicted to the study of the Scriptures." He won a place in Magdalen Hall and became a fine Greek student. About 1510 he went to Cambridge where Erasmus was Professor of Greek from 1509 to 1514. Here he remained under the influence of Erasmus, the foremost Hellenist of the age, till 1520. He was there in 1516 when the Greek New Testament of Erasmus was published. Erasmus (Green's *History of the English People*, 1st ed., p. 308) had said at Cambridge: "I long for the day when the husbandman shall sing to himself portions of the Scriptures as he follows the plough, when the weaver shall hum them to the tune of his shuttle, when the traveller shall while away with their stories the weariness of his journey." That longing took root in the mind and heart of young Tindale. In a controversy with an opponent who said that we had better be without God's laws than the Pope's, Tindale indignantly said: "I defy the Pope and all his laws; and if God spare me I will one day make the boy that drives the plow in England to know more of Scripture than the Pope does." That purpose became the ambition of this gifted young man.

Tindale appealed to Tunstall, Bishop of London, for permission to translate the New Testament in the Bishop's palace. He was rudely repulsed, but found a friend in Humphrey Monmouth, a London merchant, who sheltered him for a year while he pushed on the work, but soon he saw that there was no safe place in all England for his work. So in 1524 Tindale fled to Hamburg to get nearer to the protection of Luther. When in 1525 he began to print at Cologne the first translation into English of the Greek New Testament ever made, Cochlæus, a bitter enemy of Luther, informed on Tindale to the authorities at Cologne who stopped the work. Then Tindale fled to Worms with some of the sheets and got the book printed by the end of 1525. Early in 1526 copies were smuggled into England in sacks of flour, barrels, any way. The people eagerly devoured them while the bishops burned all that they could seize and stirred up Henry VIII, in spite of his independence of the Pope, against Tindale's work. But Packington, an English merchant of Antwerp, bought up whole editions and sold them to Tunstall to burn while Tindale took the money to print more. He translated his New Testament from the Greek New Testament of Erasmus. He put in controversial notes that were afterwards omitted. He went to work on the Old Testament and did a good deal of it (the Pentateuch and Jonah). But in 1534 he was arrested and carried to Vilvorde Castle near Brussels by officers of Emperor Charles V. On October 6, 1536 he was condemned and strangled and burned, as he prayed: "Lord, open the King of England's eyes." The enemies of the English Bible seemed victorious. But he laughs best who laughs last. In God's own way the work of Tindale was used for the later versions.

From Coverdale to the Great Bible

Tindale won his fight though his enemies burned him. He had created a desire for the English Bible that could not be stopped. In 1535 Miles Coverdale published a complete English Bible, the first complete Bible in English. Coverdale was a friend of Cromwell and More as well as of Tindale. He was supported by the ecclesiastics and yet was sympathetic with Tindale. So in 1537 two editions of his Bible appeared "set forth with the King's most gracious license." That was a victory for Tindale since Coverdale's New Testament was based mainly on the work of Tindale. It is sometimes called the Treacle Bible because of

EARLY ENGLISH BIBLES

that word in Jer. 8:22. He was not a great scholar like Tindale, but he knew how to use other men and to work with men better than Tindale did. So, he incorporated Tindale's wonderful work. Another friend of Tindale, John Rogers, an Oxford graduate of 1525, was the heir of the unpublished translation by Tindale of Joshua to 2 Chronicles. So he prepared an edition of the Bible with Tindale's translation from Genesis to 2 Chronicles, with Coverdale's translation for the rest of the Old Testament and the Apocrypha, and with Tindale's last revision of the New Testament. He added introductory matter and some marginal notes and published it under the name of "Thomas Matthew" to conceal his connection with Tindale. Cranmer and Cromwell obtained the approval of King Henry VIII for this version. This was in 1537. Eleven years before copies of Tindale's New Testament had been publicly burned by the order of the Bishop of London in St. Paul's churchyard. And now under the name of Matthew's Bible his work was published with the King's approval. This Matthew's Bible was the real basis of our present English Bible. All other versions worked on it as the basis. Rogers was burned at Smithfield in 1555. Taverner's Bible in 1539 was a slightly revised reprint of the Matthew's Bible with the polemical notes toned down. There were now two English Bibles with the King's approval (Coverdale's and Matthew's). Cromwell seemed uneasy lest the Tindale translation produced by Rogers under the name of Thomas Mathew might arouse opposition. So he persuaded Coverdale to go to work upon another. He secured scholars to bring the Old Testament portion more in harmony with the Hebrew and Latin texts of the Complutensian Polyglot. The result was called the Great Bible because of its magnificent proportions and Cranmer's Bible because of his support. It was in black letter like the others, but had no notes. Coverdale had gone to Paris to print it, but escaped to England with the printing press, the type, and the printers, though the Bibles printed in Paris were seized. In 1539 the Great Bible appeared under royal approval and it was ordered to be set up in a convenient place where people could read it. Some of these Bibles were chained to pillars in the churches so that they would always be there for the people to read. Sometimes people found these Bibles more interesting than the sermons. On the title page of this Great Bible it is stated that at the King's Command Cuthbert the Bishop of Durham had perused the work. This Bishop of Durham is Cuthbert Tunstall, former Bishop of London, who had ordered copies of Tindale's New Testament to be burned. But the Great Bible was in reality only a revised edition of the Matthew's Bible which had used all of Tindale's work. It was a great day for England when the Bible in English was open to all the people.

The Geneva Bible

Whittingham, a brother-in-law of Calvin, in 1557 produced a translation of the New Testament at Geneva. The Old Testament appeared in 1560 with the help of other scholars. It was brought out under the influence of Calvin and had fuller notes than any other. It was the first translation to drop the black letter for the Roman type. Like its predecessors it was a revision of the work of Tindale, though a more careful piece of work than even Cranmer's Great Bible. It became the most popular Bible that England had ever had and held its place for seventy-five years, slowly giving way at last to the King James Version. It was the first English Bible to recognize the divisions into verses by Robert Stephens in 1550. It was also the first to omit the Old Testament Apocrypha and it left off Paul's name from the Epistle to the Hebrews. It also used italics for all words not a part of the original text. The sharp notes in this Bible had much to do with giving rise to the King James Version. It is also called the Breeches Bible because of the translation of Gen. 3: 7.

The Bishops' Bible

Henry VIII died in 1547. Edward VI reigned till 1553 and thirty-five editions of the New Testament and thirteen of the Old were printed during this period. The Bible was open to all during Edward's short reign. But Bloody Mary (1553–8) changed all this. Cranmer and Rogers were burned at the stake. There were many others who gave up their lives (at least 400) and some fled to Geneva. Copies of the Bible were again burned. But in 1558 Queen Elizabeth took the side of Protestantism and of the open Bible. So Archbishop Parker took steps in 1563–4 for a revision of the Great Bible. He was the general editor with many assistants, nine of whom were bishops. Hence it was called the Bishops' Bible. It was finished in 1568. It did not have the formal approval of Queen Elizabeth, but she did not oppose it. The work was of unequal value, better in the New than in the Old Testament. It had ecclesiastical sanction, but it was ponderous and inferior to the Geneva Bible which had become the Bible of the Puritans. The Bishops' Bible did displace the Great Bible, but it could not set aside the Geneva Bible.

The Douai Bible

The Roman Catholics from the days of Wycliffe had bitterly opposed the efforts to put the Bible into English for the people. But now in self-defence they had to do something to counteract the Geneva Bible which was so popular. William Allen, an Oxford man, planned this version, and it was carried out under the direction of Gregory Martin, another Oxford man. The New Testament was printed in 1582 at Rheims and the Old Testament at Douai by 1610. It is translated "from the authenticall Latin." Slight use was made of anything but the Latin Vulgate and it is extremely literal and makes awkward English. There were three reprints of the New Testament and one of the Old Testament between 1582 and 1750. It was very little used as is plain.

The King James Version

James I began his reign in 1603. He summoned in 1604 a conference to meet in Hampton Court to consider complaints from the Puritans. Dr. Reynolds, President of Corpus Christi College, Oxford, was the leader of the Puritans. He complained of the need of a new translation of the Bible because of "a most

EARLY ENGLISH BIBLES

corrupted translation" in the Prayerbook. The examples that he cited were from the Great Bible and the Bishops' Bible. It so happened that James I had taken some interest in Bible study and translation and very much disliked the Geneva Bible because of some of the notes in it. So he took up the idea and appointed fifty-four to make a new translation. Only forty-seven of them are now known to us. Perhaps the other seven did not really act. From 1604 to 1607 the time was spent in preliminary arrangements and in doing private study for the work. There were six groups of the revisers, two at Westminster, two at Oxford, two at Cambridge. They were competent men and went at their work seriously. There were fifteen rules to guide them in their work. One was that the Bishops' Bible should be followed as far as possible in accordance with the truth of the original, though the others could be followed. That meant that Tindale's work was the real basis followed. There were six men, one from each group, who passed on the final result. There were to be no marginal notes at all except the explanation of Hebrew or Greek words. The revisers used the current Hebrew Bibles and Beza's edition of the Stephens (Erasmus) Greek New Testament with the aid of the Latin Vulgate. It was a wonderful piece of work, but had a pedantic and tedious preface. There were two folio editions in 1611 and one duodecimo edition of the New Testament. Dr. Scrivener speaks of the innumerable errors of the press. Most of these were gradually weeded out, but others came in. The Vinegar Bible (1717) has "vinegar" for "vineyard" in Luke 20 (heading of the column). The "Wicked Bible" leaves out "not" in the seventh commandment (Exodus 20:14), perhaps from deviltry on the part of the printer. But no two editions are alike and in six editions 24,000 variations have been found in text and punctuation. "We have a standard translation, but not a standard text" (Schaff, *op. cit.*, p. 325).

The King James Version was not authorized by the King or Parliament, so far as any record goes, though it went forth with the silent approval of both state and church. But it did not have an easy time. It was ridiculed by Dr. Broughton, a great Hebraist, who was jealous because he was not one of the company of revisers. And even John Lightfoot thought none too well of it. Roman Catholics accused it of falsifying the Scriptures. Arminians thought it too Calvinistic. Puritans disliked the use of "church," "bishop," "ordain," "Easter," etc. And it had to contend with a powerful rival, the Geneva Bible, which continued to be reprinted till the middle of the seventeenth century.

It was not the work of one man, but of many minds. "For the idiom and vocabulary Tindale deserves the greatest credit, for the melody and harmony Coverdale, for scholarship and accuracy the Geneva version" (Schaff, *op. cit.*, p. 338). It is impossible to exaggerate the part played by this wonderful translation on the life of the Anglo-Saxon peoples on five continents. F. W. Faber, the Roman Catholic, says: "It lives on the ear like a music that can never be forgotten, like the sound of church bells, which the convert hardly knows how he can forego."

But the revisers of the King James Version did not have access to the oldest and best manuscripts of the Greek New Testament that are now accessible to scholars. They did not know the Hebrew and the Greek as well as modern philologians. Hundreds of words used in the Authorized Version have changed their meanings through the centuries. New translations have become a necessity in spite of the charm and grandeur of the King James Version. In 1911 the tercentenary of the Authorized Version was celebrated by the issuance of the 1911 Bible, as it was called, being an effort to bring the King James Version up to date by the minimum of necessary changes. But it was done too hurriedly, too many changes were made, and it failed to get a hearing. Such a revision could have been made by a genius like Tindale that would have preserved the music of the Old English and the phrases that have become a part of the life of five continents.

CHAPTER XI

THE REVISED NEW TESTAMENT AFTER FORTY YEARS

The Canterbury Revision of the New Testament was published in England on Tuesday, May 17, and in the United States on Friday, May 20, 1881. The Old Testament appeared in 1885. It is now forty-five years since this great event, for it was a great event, the goal of many struggles and hopes. It is time to take stock of the outcome of the years that have passed. It may be interesting to note that the last edition of the Bishops' Bible was 1606, five years before the King James Version of 1611, though the New Testament in this version was reprinted as late as 1618. But the Geneva Bible continued to be printed in folio in England till 1616, and in quarto in Amsterdam till 1633, and in folio till 1644. The notes of the Geneva Bible were added to the King James Version in folio in 1679, and reprinted as late as 1715. But in the end the King James Version won the field, and held it till 1881. How is it now with the Revised New Testament?

It cannot be said that the Revision of 1881 has won as complete a victory as the King James Version finally did. The conditions were not the same. Many, in fact, regarded the task of the Revised Ver-

THE REVISION AFTER FORTY YEARS

sion as an impossible one. There were two hundred and fifty years of undisputed sway behind the King James Version when the Revision challenged its supremacy. The very life of Anglo-Saxon peoples on five continents was interlaced with this version that was precious in cottage and in palace. It was argued that the masses of Christians would not be willing to give up the wonderful version that was so dear to their hearts. It must be confessed that this prophecy has been largely verified by the event. The masses today still read the Authorized Version. The schools, ministers of culture, and many Sunday school teachers use the Revised Version (either Canterbury or American Standard Version), but the people love the King James Version.

There was abundant need for the Revision of 1881. There were undoubted defects in the King James Version, in spite of its marvellous English and its moulding influence on the language and life of the people. Time had done its inevitable work on the meaning of words. "Let" no longer means "hinder" in English. "Prevent" does not any more mean "precede." "Conversation" means "talk," not "walk." "By and by" no more means "immediately." There was a frequent loose use of prepositions and terms in the Authorized translation that no modern scholar could indorse in the light of modern philology. The Greek article was wofully mistreated, largely because of the Latin Vulgate, which has no article. Variations in the translation of the same word brought confusion, as in "eternal" and "everlasting," *aionios* in Matthew 25:46. Different Greek words were rendered by the same English word, as "devil" for "demon" and "devil."

New discoveries of old Greek manuscripts had thrown a flood of light on the true text of the New Testament. The King James Version rested on a comparatively small number of late Greek manuscripts (cursives or minuscules) employed in the Textus Receptus (the Erasmus-Stephens-Beza text). These late manuscripts had various additions not found in the old and better uncials like Codex Vaticanus (B), Codex Sinaiticus (Aleph), Codex Bezæ (D), and others. The whole science of textual criticism had slowly developed and was at the service of the scholars who worked on the Revision of 1881. The two chief men in this science, Westcott and Hort, were members of the committee that worked in the Jerusalem Chamber from 1870 to 1881.

Four-fifths of the changes made by the Revision of 1881 had already been pointed out by scholars in various books. Half-learned ministers had begun to spend much time in the pulpit mending the King James Version, to the confusion of the congregation. Something had to be done. It was a wise step, therefore, when Bishop Wilberforce moved and Bishop Ellicott seconded the resolution in the Convocation of Canterbury, on February 10, 1870, calling for a Revision of the King James Version.

This action of the Church of England authorities led to the appointment of an Old Testament Committee (twenty-seven) and a New Testament Committee (twenty-four). Of these, thirty-six were Church of England scholars, and the other eighteen Non-Conformists. An American Committee was added, which worked together with the British Committee. These scholars aimed to produce a Revision, not a new translation. But there were many men of many minds. In 1871, Lightfoot (in connection with Trench and Ellicott) published a valuable work showing the need of a revision of the New Testament, *The Revision of the English Version of the New Testament*. It was a personal statement, but it made out a complete case for a revision.

The New Testament Committee included the greatest scholars of Britain. The American Committee was composed of scholars within easy reach of New York for the monthly meetings, and that excluded some of the ablest men in the United States, including John A. Broadus, then of Greenville, S. C., the ablest New Testament scholar in America. The American Committee made a great many corrections and changes not acceptable to the British Committee. The most important of these were printed in an Appendix at the end, as well as in the footnotes, till 1895 (fourteen years), when the Appendix was dropped. Then the American Committee felt free to produce the American Standard Version (1901), which incorporated the ideas of the American Committee, and which has a great vogue in the United States.

The reception of the Canterbury Revision was exceedingly enthusiastic and hearty, especially in the United States. Papers in the United States in 1881 published the whole of the New Testament. Newsboys cried, "Here's your New Testament, just out." Both the Oxford and the Cambridge Presses had orders for a million copies before publication. The sale in New York was as great as that in London. People literally bought the Revision by the millions. The reception in America was even more cordial than in England, though the work was mainly done by British scholars.

At first many ministers hesitated to use the Revision in the pulpit. It made its way more rapidly among Sunday school teachers and among ministers of culture and in theological seminaries. But objections arose in many places against the Revision. Some greatly objected to the changes in text, even where the evidence was overwhelming, as in the omission of the three heavenly witnesses in 1 John 5:7, 8, a manifestly spurious passage, and the change of "God" to "he who" in 1 Timothy 3:16, a return to the original text. Others missed familiar phrases, and felt that many of the changes were needless. The result was exasperating, and many refused or failed to get the benefit of the real improvements made in a great many ways, because of long attachment to the King James Version. The London *Times* of May 20, 1881, welcomed the Revision, but doubted its final victory. "As we shall see, there are difficulties connected with a conservative revision of the existing translation of the Greek Testament that are practically insuperable." That judgment is correct, and yet the Revision has been eminently worth while.

The Revision had undoubtedly popularized real Bible study. Thousands who have continued to employ the King James Version for devotional reading because of sentimental or literary attachment have yet been willing to use the Revised Version for study of sermons or the Sunday school lessons. Most of the schools that employ the New Testament have introduced the Revised Version, and in the United States, since 1901, the American Standard Version. The two versions have gone on side by side, like the Geneva Bible and the Authorized Version in the seventeenth century, with the difference that the King James Version shows no signs of a final surrender to the Revised. The two versions still sell in enormous quantities, the King James probably leading. But a generation of young people have grown up familiar with the Revision. Ministers no longer apologize for reading it in the pulpit. Sunday school publications use it alone or in connection with the King James. Will the Revised Version finally displace the King James Version? That is a hard question to answer. Some version will, if the English language keeps on changing. Either the Revised Version or some other will do so.

There are undoubted advances in the Revision over the King James Version. It has a better Greek text behind it, as any scholar can see for himself who will compare the Textus Receptus with "*The Greek Testament with the Readings Adopted by the Revisers of the Authorized Version,*" by Palmer (1881). A still better edition is Souter's *Novum Testamentum Graece* (1910), which gives the Greek Text used by the Revisers, with variations of important manuscripts. In 1892 Whitney wrote two volumes on *The Revisers' Greek Text*, in which he makes a careful study of the chief changes of the text. Schaff gives a select list of improved renderings in the Revised Version in his *Companion to the*

Greek Testament and English Version (3d ed., 1889, pp. 434 to 468), where one may see for himself many of the real advantages of the Revised Version, like "Be not anxious," instead of "Take no thought" (Matt. 6:25); "strain out the gnat," for "strain at a gnat" (Matt. 23:24); "our lamps are going out," for "our lamps are gone out" (Matt. 25:8); "see with how large letters," instead of "how large a letter" (Gal. 6:11); "The love of money is a root of all kinds of evil," instead of "the root of all evil" (1 Tim. 6:10); the use of "its" for "his" (Matt. 5:13).

Is the American Standard Version superior to the Canterbury Revision? For America, yes. The American Committee objected to the use of "Saint" with the titles of the books. They do not like "which" for "who," "be" for "are," "wot" and "wist" for "know" and "knew," "Ghost" for "Spirit," "devils" for "demons," "corn" for "grain," the use of "God forbid" where "God" does not occur, as in Galatians 6:14, and many other points that reflect American feeling and usage.

There was more timidity among the British Revisers, and more courage among the Americans. Some of the British scholars openly advocated nearly all the changes proposed by the American Committee. In some instances custom prevailed against truth. But a clean bill of health cannot be given to the work of the American Committee, for in Titus 2:13 they changed "Our great God and Saviour Jesus Christ" to "the great God and our Saviour Jesus Christ," whereas the Greek idiom plainly calls for the former translation, a definite statement of the Deity of Jesus

Christ by Paul, as I have shown in *The Minister and His Greek New Testament*. They fail also to see the significance of the one Greek article in 2 Peter 1:1, and have "our God and *the* Saviour Jesus Christ," instead of "our God and Saviour Jesus Christ," as the Greek has it.

As the case stands today, the American Standard Version has the field in the United States among those who want the Revision, while it is not allowed to circulate in Britain. There are practically two Revised Versions, neither of which can drive the other off the field.

Then there is a lack of unanimity on the subject that leads many to fall back on the King James Version, who might otherwise have accepted a translation agreed upon by both branches of the English speaking peoples. Modern Christians, however, do have the advantage of both the Canterbury and the American Revisions, and are learning how to use both with profit. The effect of this situation is to stimulate individual study on the part of many who welcome the many individual translations. The day may come when there will be so many translations in use that one more effort will be made to produce one translation that will be acceptable to Anglo-Saxons all over the world. That solution will be more difficult now than in 1611, more difficult now than in 1881. Today Canada, Australia, New Zealand, South Africa, would lay claim to a share in such an undertaking by Britain and America. "One of the adverse critics naively confesses that till the year 1882 he was happily ignorant of the existence of any eminent biblical scholars and critics in America" (Schaff, *Companion to the Greek Testament and English Version*, p. 491). Happily such provincial prejudice is gone, and coöperation among Anglo-Saxon scholars would be now possible and profitable. But there is no sign of such an international effort on the horizon. As things are, one can thank God for the King James Version and its history, for the Canterbury Revision, for the American Standard Version, and for all others that will help modern men to get a better knowledge of the message of God to men. M. B. Riddle in *The Story of the Revised New Testament* gives the main facts in an interesting way.

CHAPTER XII

RECENT TRANSLATIONS OF THE NEW TESTAMENT

Dissatisfaction with the standard translations of the New Testament has led to a number of individual versions with varying degrees of merit. The antique charm of the King James Version fails to satisfy those who wish a rendering in modern English and based on a more exact Greek text. Many feel that the Canterbury Revision went too far not to go farther. It is neither a mere revision nor an independent translation. The American Standard Version does go farther, but shows strange inconsistencies at times, with occasional relapses into the text of the King James Version, as in Romans 5:1, "we have peace," instead of, "let us have peace," of the Canterbury Revision. More exactly it is, "let us keep on having peace" (linear action, present active subjunctive, not aorist). Besides, there seems to be no prospect of a standard version accepted by scholars of both England and America. Hence translations by individual scholars are having quite a vogue and there seems to be no sign of a decrease of interest in such efforts.

No one of these individual translations has any chance of winning the victory over the standard versions for general use. However, ministers freely use in the pulpit any one of them as they wish. But no one scholar can please all denominations and all classes of readers on both sides of the sea by his own renderings, however brilliant and suggestive they may be. There are, to be sure, advantages in a translation of the New Testament by one man, as is seen in the work by Wycliffe or of Tindale, provided only he be a man of real scholarship and of spiritual insight. If in addition he has genius and style, the work may be superior to the resultant translation of a number of men where compromise has to play so large a part. But courage must be consonant with delicate taste and tact and absence of mere whimsicalities and objectionable idiosyncrasies. Personality is power, and an individual translation illustrates this fact finely, but it must not be overdone.

The ideal is to produce a translation that will best reproduce the mind of the original language, that will convey the same concept to the reader. That is a difficult thing to do. The Greek word itself may have several connotations that shade away from each other. In any given instance that precise shade must be caught and reproduced by an English word with various shades of meaning, any one of which may be apprehended by various readers. It is precisely for this reason that it is impossible to make an exact and full translation from the Greek New Testament into any language. The thing has never been done, and it will never be done by any man or by any group of men. There are delicate nuances in particles, prepositions, articles, pronouns, cases, tenses, voices, modes, infinitives, and participles that find no precise parallel in English. But the masses of modern Christians do not know the Greek New Testament and never will know it. If they cannot or will not have access to the full New Testament meaning in the *Koiné*, they are at least entitled to as good a translation as modern scholarship can make. Hence translation is a necessity.

Even if the British and American scholars had agreed upon every point in 1881, there would still today be ample reason for new translations of the New Testament. Besides the discovery of new manuscripts like the Washington Codex and the Sinaitic Syriac, great advance has been made in the knowledge of New Testament philology. Comparative philology has been applied to the grammar of the Greek New Testament in a scientific way. Papyri discoveries in Egypt have thrown a flood of light upon our knowledge of the language of the Greek New Testament, which is in the vernacular *Koiné* of the First Century A.D. with touches of the literary *Koiné* in places. All this is now set forth in new grammars and lexicons that make the new knowledge accessible to all. The scholars in 1881 did not possess the knowledge of the language of the New Testament that is now available. Hence those today who undertake to apply the new knowledge to the translation of the New Testament deserve our gratitude. Perfection is not to be expected in any translation. One will excel in one point, another in another, each according to his own gift. It is advantageous to have several of those translations and compare them with each other and, still better, with the Greek.

The Twentieth Century New Testament first appeared in 1898 (Fleming H. Revell Co., New York, for this country). That is to say, Part I was published in that year, including the five historical books (Gospels and Acts). Part II covered Paul's letters to the Churches, and was published in 1900. Part III embraced the rest of the New Testament, and followed in 1901. This translation was made from the Greek text of Westcott and Hort by a group of English scholars who first put it forth as a tentative translation and invited criticisms. There have been a large number of editions, and the work was done with decided ability.

Chapters and verses appear in the margin, and the paragraphs have headings set into the side of the text in black type. Quotation marks are used, and quotations from the Old Testament are placed in italics with the references in footnotes. An outline of each book is incorporated into the text. The order of the books is changed, but not into a chronological arrangement. Mark's Gospel is placed first, followed by Matthew, Luke, John, and Acts.

The Pauline Epistles are divided into groups, but not on the chronological basis. Group I includes First and Second Thessalonians; Group II, Romans, First and Second Corinthians, Galatians (note place); Group III, Ephesians, Philippians, Colossians (putting Philippians between Ephesians and Colossians). In Part III come the Pastoral Letters (First and Second Timothy, Titus, though Second Timothy is clearly last of all), while Philemon comes last of all, with Second and Third John (Personal Letters), whereas it clearly belongs in time with Colossians and Ephesians.

The General Letters include Hebrews, James, First

John, First and Second Peter, Jude, Revelation. This arrangement is correct topically, save that Hebrews is not a general epistle.

The work would have been much improved by giving the Pauline Epistles in real chronological order. The translation is into modern vernacular English, dignified, but fresh and often with happy turns of expression that challenge one's attention. The peril of all old translations is that one will read the words with a wandering mind. The new translation compels attention and that is a great gain, provided, of course, the translation faithfully renders the original Greek. *The Twentieth Century Translation* has decided merits, with some obvious drawbacks. It was worth doing, and it still has a place for service. It is a new translation, not a revision and, though a free translation, not a paraphrase.

The New Testament in Modern Speech (The Pilgrim Press, Boston) was made in 1902 by R. F. Weymouth, D.Litt., Fellow of University College, London. It is "an idiomatic translation into everyday English" from the text of *The Resultant Greek Testament* edited by the same scholar (1892). This work has been found very helpful by many precisely because the author endeavored to get away from Tindale's immortal work, which has dominated even the Canterbury and American Standard Versions (Preface, Page v). He has sought to avoid both slang and literary elegance, while not afraid to retain old words if they are not obsolete. The author disclaims any desire to supplant the standard translations, but seeks only to furnish a running commentary to go side by side with the Authorized and Revised Versions. He is not always as literal in his renderings as the Revised Version or as Darby's New Testament, which he likes still better. He hopes that his own work may contribute something towards that new standard version that will come some day.

Dr. Weymouth had already written a pamphlet, "On Rendering Into English the Greek Aorist and Perfect," in which he pointed out the impossibility of an exact translation of these tenses into English. But he did take unusual pains to do justice to the Greek tenses. Chapters and verses are put on the margin. Headings to the paragraphs appear in black type in insets. Quotations from the Old Testament appear in capital letters with references, while quotation marks are used for conversation or speeches. There are valuable footnotes that give explanations of many of the renderings.

It is a very fine piece of work and many men have found it very helpful. The author succeeded in his aim. He has produced a modern translation of a high order in dignified vernacular that is reasonably faithful to the Greek text. His Greek text is called Resultant, because for the most part it represents that where modern editors agree.

I have passed by an earlier translation, of 1891, called the "Improved Edition" of that made by the American Bible Union. This translation was made by three Baptist scholars (John A. Broadus, Alvah Hovey, and Henry G. Weston), and has a great deal of merit. But it was published under denominational auspices (American Baptist Publication Society, Philadelphia), and necessarily has had a limited circulation.

A New Translation, by Dr. James Moffatt (Hodder and Stoughton, London; George H. Doran Co., New York) appeared in 1913 and has had a great vogue on both sides of the Atlantic. It is translated from Von Soden's text rather than from that of Westcott and Hort, with some special rearrangements of the material, as in the Gospel of John and the Epistle of James. By this means English readers can get the benefit of Von Soden's idea of the Greek text, but it raises disputed questions in several places, especially in Matthew 1:16, where Von Soden follows the Sinaitic Syriac and the Ferrar Group of Greek minuscules in giving the text, "Joseph begat Jesus," which reading contradicts Matthew 1:18-25 in the same manuscripts, unless the word "begat" is used in a general sense. Again, Dr. Moffatt accepts the suggestion of Dr. J. Rendel Harris that "Enoch" has dropped out of the text in 1 Peter 3:19. That emendation would solve the problem of the preaching to the spirits in prison by Enoch instead of Christ.

Without question this work by Moffatt is brilliant and stimulating to an unusual degree. He is a thorough Greek scholar in touch with modern linguistic research and with a fresh and virile style and a quick and lively imagination. But it is a chastened style that does not run riot, though the new renderings grip one's mind by their very vigor. Many of his renderings are exceedingly happy. It is small wonder that students of the New Testament have found this translation so rich with fertile suggestions. The book is in good type, with chapters and verses in the margin, but with no insets or headings. Scripture quotations appear in italics. The book has had many editions, pocket size and limp leather back, and in parallel columns with the King James Version. Moffatt's new translation constantly sends the reader who knows the Greek New Testament back to the original, to see if his fresh way of putting the thing is in accord with the text. This is wholly to the good, and is not the least of the merits of his translation.

As early as 1901 Dr. Moffatt made a new translation for his *Historical New Testament*, in which the books were printed in the order of writing, as Dr. Moffatt understood them. But that translation had nothing to do with his *New Translation*. In the *New Translation* the books are printed in the same order as in the standard versions.

In the early autumn of 1923 Dr. E. J. Goodspeed (the University of Chicago Press, Chicago) produced a very readable American translation. His point is that the *Twentieth Century New Testament*, Weymouth's *New Testament in Modern Speech*, and Moffatt's *New Translation* are all done by British scholars, with the inevitable result that phrases familiar to British ears are not readily understood by Americans. He thinks that it is time to have an American translation by an American scholar for American readers in their own vernacular. There is point in this view beyond a doubt, for American vernacular has steadily drifted away from the British on many points. Dr. Goodspeed does not aim to give American slang at all, but only thoroughly understandable vernacular for the business man who reads papers and magazines.

RECENT TRANSLATIONS

The ambition of Dr. Goodspeed is to get the New Testament read by the average American. It is a laudable aim, as any one can see.

Dr. Goodspeed is thoroughly equipped on the linguistic side as Professor of Biblical and Patristic Greek in the University of Chicago. He is a specialist in the study of the papyri and in the textual criticism of the New Testament. He follows the Greek text of Westcott and Hort, except that he omits the passages marked as interpolations by Westcott and Hort. He departs from the text of Westcott and Hort in John 19:29; Acts 19:28, 34; James 1:17; 3:6; Revelation 13:1. He has adopted some of the emendations proposed by Hort in "Notes on Select Readings." Like Moffatt, he follows the suggestion of J. Rendel Harris to insert Enoch in 1 Peter 3:19.

Dr. Goodspeed is in thorough sympathy with the new light on the language of the New Testament from the papyri discoveries and comparative philology, and has applied the new knowledge to his translation. The book is well printed. The chapters and verses are indicated at the bottom of the page only. The quotation marks, punctuation, and paragraphing are just like a modern book of fiction. It is an eminently readable translation. Dr. Goodspeed seeks to tempt men to read one of the books at a sitting, and to understand what they read without an interpreter to tell them. One can find flaws in this as in all translations. He prints "holy Spirit" thus, — why I do not know. Instead of "justify" in Romans he uses "make upright," which suits in some places much better than it does in others where it means "declare upright."

The reception given Dr. Goodspeed's translation has been phenomenal. Some newspapers have carried it as a serial. Others have written editorials condemning its vernacular idiom. But the book has had an unusual circulation, and promises to make the New Testament read by the masses more than ever. That will certainly be a blessing.

In 1923 another translation by an American, Dr. William G. Ballantine, appeared. It is entitled *The Riverside New Testament: A Translation from the Original Greek into the English of Today* (Houghton, Mifflin Company, Boston). Dr. Ballantine does not profess to put his version into distinctly American vernacular, as Dr. Goodspeed does, but into "the living English of today." He is not unaware of the work of others. Originality has been neither sought nor shunned. He owes much to the King James Version, the Revised Version, the Twentieth Century New Testament, Weymouth's New Testament in Modern Speech, Moffatt's New Translation. He considers them all of great merit, but feels that each one leaves something tc be desired. So he proceeds to do it. That is the way that progress is made. Others will find defects in *The Riverside New Testament*, though it has merits of its own. Instead of "justify" he gives "account righteous," which is better than Goodspeed's "make upright."

Dr. Ballantine says that he had been getting ready for this translation all his life, so that it was not a sudden impulse with him. It was a sense of obligation that drove him on. He follows the Nestle Greek text in the main, as Goodspeed the Westcott and Hort, Moffatt the Von Soden, Weymouth the Resultant Greek text, the Twentieth Century the Westcott and Hort. Because of this fact English readers can form some idea of the variations in the Greek text of various modern editions of the Greek New Testament. Dr. Ballantine gives the chapters, but not the verses. There are no headings and no notes of any kind. Quotation marks are used, and paragraphs, but the text is not broken up into dialogue form, as in Goodspeed's American translation. The print is attractive, and the book deserves well of the public. Dr. Ballantine calls the King James Version "three hundred years behind the times," and, like Dr. Goodspeed, is not afraid of the "ghost of King James."

America seems to be making up for lost time in translations of the New Testament. The American Baptist Publication Society (Philadelphia) celebrated in 1924 the first hundred years of its work, partly by the *Centenary Translation of the New Testament*, by Helen Barrett Montgomery, A.M., D.H.L., LL.D. Here we have an American translation, and by a woman of scholarship. She keeps the chapters and verses in the margin. The book is printed like a modern book, with quotation marks. The Old Testament quotations are in italics. There are chapter headings and topics also for each subdivision, in black type, at the head of the paragraph. The Scripture references are in footnotes. Mrs. Montgomery endeavors to produce a translation into "the language of everyday life, that does not depart too much from the translations already familiar and beloved." She has in mind the ordinary reader with only average education. The book is printed in handy size for pocket or hand-bag, and is sold at a cheap price. Some of her renderings are striking, and the translation runs along with smoothness and grace.

In 1923 George H. Doran Co. (New York) published my *Translation of Luke's Gospel with Grammatical Notes*. The Notes come at the end, and explain and justify the renderings of various tenses, prepositions, cases, etc. The translation itself is into idiomatic English, with the view of reproducing as far as possible the delicate nuances of the Greek idioms not preserved in the usual translation. The book is designed for those who are willing to take time enough to understand the Gospel of Luke in all its wondrous beauty. Chapters and verses are in the margin. The book is printed like a modern book, with headings for the main paragraphs, with quotation marks, and with Scripture quotations in italics. The text used is that of Westcott and Hort.

Thus it will be seen that each of the individual translations brings out some point not emphasized by the others. They are all helpful if one does not know the Greek. Some of them are specially useful to those who do know the Greek. They all testify to a revival of interest in the reading of the New Testament. The Bible is still the best seller. New Translations will continue to come out. Let them come. Let them be read. There is room for them all.

CHAPTER XIII

WRONG CHAPTER AND VERSE DIVISIONS IN THE NEW TESTAMENT

It is curious what slaves most of us are to custom. We quickly enslave ourselves to our accustomed routine. The Revised Version of the New Testament stirred one pious brother to remark that the King James Version was good enough for the Apostle Paul and it was good enough for him. And yet for nearly fifty years it was not certain whether the King James Version or the Geneva would win the day. When Erasmus published in 1516 his first Greek New Testament, he printed side by side with the Greek text a Latin translation and some notes. In his edition of 1527 he put in also the Latin Vulgate which had for centuries held the field in the West. But this Latin Vulgate of Jerome for many years met a storm of abuse from those who preferred the Old Latin versions. The King James Version which the Revised Version challenged in 1881 had the verses printed separately as if each verse was a separate paragraph. The effect of this way of printing the text was to destroy all sense of connection between the verses. Each verse stood out as a thing to itself. Many people have expressed great surprise when it first dawned upon them that there was any grammatical or logical connection between the verses. Paragraph marks were indeed printed here and there, but these marks made little impression upon the average reader.

The Revised Version put both chapter and verse divisions on the margin and printed the text in paragraphs according to the sense. This courageous act of itself was enough to justify the work of the Revisers if they had done nothing else. But, when the American Standard Version appeared in 1901, the chapter and verse divisions crept back into the text, only the paragraphs were retained and the verse numbers were printed in the body of the text. This plan made the beginning and end of each verse easier to detect, but made some interruption in the easy reading of the text. Moffatt places the verses on the margin while Goodspeed drops both chapters and verses to the bottom of the page with no interruption at all to the flow of the narrative. But many good people are already troubled over this liberty with the verse divisions in the Bible. It may be worth while to recount the history of this matter.

It seems hardly necessary to state that our verse divisions come after the age of printing. They appear in no Greek manuscript. The Masoretic verses of the Old Testament were first numbered by Rabbi Isaac Nathan for use in his Hebrew Concordance, finished in 1448 and printed in 1524 at Venice. These Masoretic verses were first numbered by Arabic figures in 1509 in the *Quincuplex Psalterium*. In 1528 Sanctes Pagninus printed at Lyons a Latin translation of the whole Bible with verse divisions. "But in the Apocrypha and the New Testament his division was very different from ours, the verses being twice or three times as

WRONG CHAPTER AND VERSE DIVISIONS 151

long; and it seems to have been followed in no other edition" (Ezra Abbot, *On the Division of the Greek New Testament into Verses, Critical Essays*, 1888, p. 465).

Our New Testament verse divisions were made by Robert Stephens as he made a horse-back journey, *inter equitandum*, "while riding," from Paris to Lyons. One old commentator, after laboring with the verse divisions of Stephens, said: "I think it had been better done on his knees in the closet." It is generally supposed that Stephens did the work while riding to relieve the tedium of the long trip. If he actually did it while jogging along, it is certain that the horse gave some bumps in the wrong place. But Gregory (*Canon and Text of the New Testament*, p. 474) challenges this interpretation and thinks that all that is meant is that he made the verse divisions during the stops for rest while on the journey. "During the morning he may have rested a while at a wayside inn, and certainly at noon he will have done so. And again at night he doubtless drew out his little pocket edition and 'divided' away until it was time to sleep." Be that as it may, we know that Erasmus had no verse divisions in his Greek New Testament. Why did Stephens make his verse divisions for the edition of 1551? He had none in his previous editions of 1546, 1549, 1550 (his "royal edition"). He was at work on a Concordance of the New Testament, published by his son Henri in 1594. It was absolutely necessary to have verse divisions in order to give proper references in his concordance. So he proceeded to make verse divisions for his own convenience and for the confusion of readers of the New

Testament ever since. They do help preachers find their texts, but they hinder both preachers and people from grasping the sense of a passage.

The first use of Stephens's verses was made by him in the fourth edition of his Greek New Testament in 1551. The Greek text was a reprint of the 1550 edition Greek text with the Greek in the middle column, the Latin translation of Erasmus on the outer side, and the Latin Vulgate on the inner side of the page. The Arabic verse numbers come between the Greek and the Latin translation of Erasmus. J. Rendel Harris (*Some Notes on the Verse-Divisions of the New Testament*, Journal of Biblical Literature, 1900, Part II, p. 117 f.) shows that Stephens made the verse divisions on the Latin Vulgate New Testament which was used as a printers' copy for his Greek New Testament of 1551. In the Stephens Vulgate of 1545 there is a verse in Acts 2:19 and 20 not in the Greek or Latin of Stephens's 1551 New Testament. Hence the printer prints 19 and 20 together, for the verse on which Stephens marked it is absent. That missing verse is in the Sixtine Vulgate of 1590: *et apprehenderunt me clamantes et dicentes, Tolle inimicum nostrum*. There is another case just like it with double numeration in the Stephens New Testament of 1551. It is Acts 23:25 and 26. It is extant as the missing verse 25 in the Clementine Vulgate of 1592: *Timuit enim ne forte raperent eum Judæi, et occiderent, et ipse postea calumniam sustineret, tanquam accepturus pecuniam*. Nestle made this discovery. "Moreover, the Antwerp Polyglot of 1571 expressly says, in printing this verse from the Latin with no counterpart in Greek or Syriac; *'deest 25 versus'*"

WRONG CHAPTER AND VERSE DIVISIONS 153

(Harris, *op. cit.*, p. 117). The proof is thus plain that Stephens made his verse divisions on a Latin Vulgate New Testament and gave this to the printer to use in making the verse divisions for the Greek New Testament of 1551. No printed New Testament in Greek or Latin had these divisions before 1551, so far as any record exists.

Once started, however, it was hard to stop the innovation. In 1552 Stephens printed a French New Testament with the verse divisions, the French version of Olivetan revised by Calvin. Abbot (*op. cit.*, p. 466) gives the dates for these early editions with verse divisions. The Italian followed in 1555, Paschale's version. The first Dutch version with the verses was that by Ctematius in 1556. The first English New Testament with verse divisions was that by William Whittingham, printed at Geneva in 1557. The first whole English Bible with the verses was the Geneva Bible of 1560. The first whole Bible to have the verse divisions of Stephens was his edition of the Latin Vulgate of 1555 at Geneva (made for his Latin Concordance of the same date, 1555).

Other Greek New Testaments followed suit with the verse divisions. The Elzevir Greek New Testament of 1633, the Textus Receptus edition, was the first one that had the verses divided up, a lamentable innovation. It was bad enough to have the verse divisions at all, but this was the acme of perversity in destroying the sense. And it has kept up till 1881. "Beza deviated much more frequently from the verse divisions of Robert Stephens; and his editions had great influence in giving currency to the use of the divisions into verses, which soon became general. His variations from the divisions of Stephens were largely followed by later editors, especially by the Elzevirs, who also introduced others of their own. Others still will be found in the early modern translations" (Abbot, *Critical Essays*, p. 466). Gregory greatly deplores (*Canon and Text of the New Testament*, p. 475) the variations in different Greek New Testaments and versions. Abbot thinks that the absence of any critical examination of these variations in verse enumeration is largely due to the extreme rarity of Stephens's edition of 1551, "which has the best right to be regarded as the standard, from which an editor should not deviate in marking the beginning of a verse without noting the change, and then only for very strong reasons" (*op. cit.*, p. 467). My own experience in making references over and over again to the verses in the Greek New Testament (see my *Grammar of the Greek N. T. in the Light of Historical Research*) bears out the charge that Abbot makes. I found it exceedingly difficult to feel sure that the verse given in any text was the one accepted generally. "The want of agreement in different editions, leading of course to discrepancies in concordances, dictionaries, and other books of references, often occasions doubt and perplexity." Abbot took about fifty of the chief editions and translations of the New Testament and noted variations in the different editions. It is an astonishing list on eight large, closely-printed pages. But Abbot adds: "This list is incomplete." Gregory (*op. cit.*, p. 475) wishes that some theologian would carry on what Abbot began so well and get all the data "showing

WRONG CHAPTER AND VERSE DIVISIONS 155

where false divisions have crept in," and then that "all theologians would correct their New Testaments in whatever language according to the one standard of Estienne's (Stephens's) edition of 1551." That is a greatly desirable goal, but one hardly likely of realization.

But enough has been said to make it plain how comparatively recent the whole matter of verse divisions in the New Testament really is. My sympathies are wholly with those editors who place the numbers in the margin instead of in the text and who use paragraphs and print both the Greek and the English text in a way to help one understand the sense of the passage. The custom of verse divisions arose as a convenience for reference in the use of a concordance. It has to be kept up because of convenience today. It is a necessary evil, to be sure, but it is an evil that one has to endure, but with as many limitations as possible. One cannot resist the feeling that, if we had to have verse divisions, the thing ought to have been done by one thoroughly competent, in the first place, and by one who would take the time to do it carefully and with as much regard as possible to the sentence and the sense. It is a work of supererogation now to point out the hundreds and hundreds of verse divisions in the New Testament that try the soul of any man who loves a sentence with all its balanced and proportioned members. The work was poorly done by Robert Stephens who was a printer and not a real scholar. He did it in a hurry and in a more or less mechanical manner. It was done on the Latin Vulgate first as a printer's copy and then transferred to the Greek text. It was a late

Latin Vulgate text and a late Greek text. The critical Greek text of modern scholars has had to drop out a number of verses like Acts 8:37. But what has been done has been done and cannot now be undone. The only thing open to us now is to manage the verse divisions with as little damage to the understanding of the New Testament as possible. There is absolutely nothing sacrosanct about it. It has been of some service, but at a fearful cost to the right apprehension of the New Testament.

A few examples of poor verse divisions may suffice to make the point plain: Take 2 Timothy, for instance. A needless verse is 1:4, which breaks right into the middle of the closely-knit sentence. The same thing is true of 1:11. But a worse example is seen in 1:17 and 18 where the sense is interrupted by a full stop in the King James Version. The Revised Version has it right with a parenthesis, but no verse division is permissible here. In 2:25 the verse breaks up a clause, one half of it in verse 24 and the other half in verse 25. Verse 24 surely should end with "oppose themselves," not with "patient," with the semi-colon, not with the comma. In the same way 3:3 is a needless verse division and interrupts seriously the group of adjectives. So also 3:7 should go with 3:6. These are the flagrant instances in a short epistle where the sense is seriously interrupted by the verse paragraphs in the King James Version. Schaff (*op. cit.*, p. 237) has not put the case too strongly when he says: "The versicular division is injudicious, and breaks up the text, sometimes in the middle of a sentence, into fragments, instead of presenting it in natural sections; but it is

WRONG CHAPTER AND VERSE DIVISIONS 157

convenient for reference, and has become indispensable by long use. The English Revision judiciously combines both methods." The English Revision uses sense paragraphs with verse divisions in the margin, a much better plan that that of the American Standard Version with the Arabic numbers in the body of the paragraph.

The chapter divisions are older and do not disturb the sense so seriously and so frequently, though there are flagrant blunders here also. Our modern chapters were divided by Stephen Langton, Archbishop of Canterbury, who died in 1228. He seems to have made the chapter divisions about 1204 or 1205. Gregory (*Canon and Text of the New Testament*, p. 473) says that this division in chapters by Langton got into no Greek manuscripts of the New Testament save a few late minuscules in the West. Langton, before he became Archbishop of Canterbury, was one of the doctors of the new University of Paris who were at work on purifying the text of the Vulgate. He afterwards became the leader of the barons in their contest with King John. His chapters were put into the Latin Vulgate. The Greek manuscripts (cursives) regularly had the Greek chapters while a very few of them, as already stated, had these Latin chapters of Langton, and a few (cursives) had both the Greek and the Latin chapters. About 1243 Hugo of St. Caro with a number of other learned men produced a concordance to the Latin Vulgate which used the chapters of Langton with seven other divisions in each chapter except the short chapter indicated by the letters A B C D E F G. These letters appear on the margin of the Stephens-

Erasmus Vulgate New Testament of 1545, next to the Vulgate. The Langton chapters are indicated by Roman letters. In the Stephens-Langton Vulgate New Testament of 1555 the A B C D E F G divisions and the Stephens Arabic verse enumeration occur, but the Arabic numbers occur in the text. In the Stephens Greek New Testament of 1551 only the Arabic verse divisions occur. The Langton chapter divisions are undoubtedly useful, though some are too long and some are too short and others break into the middle of a sense paragraph. It is easy for the average reader to run through the Revised New Testament and note some of these interruptions of the paragraph. A case in point is Matthew 10:1, which belongs in sense with 9:38. Another is Matthew 20:1 which cuts right into the speech of Jesus in reply to Peter. Matthew 26 is a very long chapter (75 verses) like Luke 1 (80 verses). Mark 9:1 clearly belongs to the preceding paragraph. In Acts 7:1 the chapter division breaks right into the trial of Stephen. Acts 8:1a belongs to the preceding paragraph (bad verse division also). Acts 22:30 surely should be 23:1, 2 Corinthians 2:1 breaks into the paragraph, as is true of 2 Corinthians 6:1 and 7:1. The same thing is true of Colossians 4:1. One of the very worst chapter divisions is Hebrews 12:1, which separates Jesus from the list of heroes of faith in chapter II. Surely the new chapter had better begin at 12:4. And Revelation 22:1 ought to start at 22:6 and not cut into the wonderful pictures of heaven. These examples are enough to show the immense advantage of the paragraph divisions according to sense over the fixed chapter divisions of Langton. And yet we are

WRONG CHAPTER AND VERSE DIVISIONS 159

shut up now to the actual use of these mechanical chapters.

But there were chapter divisions long before Langton. The Greek chapters (κεφάλαια) are very old, how old we do not know, but they do not correspond at all with those made by Langton for the Latin Vulgate. It is not known who made the large Greek chapters. Our oldest Greek documents have these chapter divisions on the margin. In fact, Codex Vaticanus (B) gives two separate systems of chapters for Acts, Paul's Epistles, and the Catholic Epistles. Euthalius is not the author of these sections. He merely applied a system already old for the church lessons. The Apocalypse received no chapter division, so far as known, apart from that in the commentary of Andrew of Cæsarea in Cappadocia, a very artificial arrangement. For the Gospels Clement of Alexandria spoke of pericopes (περικοπαί), Tertullian of *capitula*, Dionysius of Alexandria of κεφάλαια. Origen used περί for sections. The τίτλοι found in A C N R Z are interesting because the titles of the chapters appear in tables at the beginning of each Gospel or at the top of the page. These Greek chapters number 68 for Matthew, 48 for Mark, 83 for Luke, and 18 for John. They vary greatly in length. In Matthew 55 there are only a dozen lines, while 56 has over ninety.

There was a still further effort made to enable the reader to refer from one Gospel to another. This arrangement is called the Eusebian (Ammonian) sections and canons. The plan of Ammonius was to write the parallel sections beside each other. But Eusebius made sections or little chapters in each Gospel

(355 for Matthew, 233 for Mark, 342 for Luke, 232 for John). Then he had ten canons. The first contains a list where all four Gospels agree. The second has the passages where Matthew, Mark and Luke agree, the third where Matthew, Luke, and John agree, the fourth where Matthew, Mark, and John agree. Then come sections where two Gospels agree and finally the tenth canon has passages where each Gospel stands alone. It was an ingenious scheme and was found very useful. Eusebius put on the margin in red ink the number of the canon in which the passage is found. The reader could turn to the number of the canon and then to the Gospel or Gospels referred to by the numbers. It was a harmony of the Gospels in skeleton form and served a useful purpose.

But we are now under the regime of Langton's chapters and of Stephens's verses and can only make the best of it. We owe it to all students and readers of the New Testament to throw as few difficulties in their way as possible when they turn to the New Testament for light and leading. One can find a full presentation of the facts about the chapters in Gregory's *Prolegomena* (pp. 140–166) to Tischendorf's *Novum Testamentum Græce* (editio octava) and of the verses also (pp. 166–182) where he gives chapter XX of Ezra Abbot's *Critical Essays* with his invaluable data. Each reader today is supposed to be on his guard against the mechanical chapters and verses which, like barnacles, have fastened upon the New Testament.

The division into chapters and verses was objected to as long ago as John Locke (died 1704), who said in his *Essay for the Understanding of St. Paul's Epistles by*

Consulting St. Paul Himself "The dividing of them into Chapters and Verses, as we have done, whereby they are so chop'd and minc'd, and as they are now Printed, stand so broken and divided, that not only the Common People take the Verses usually for distinct Aphorisms, but even Men of more advanc'd Knowledge in reading them, lose very much of the strength and force of the Coherence, and the Light that depends on it." But a habit is a habit. If we can get people to read the New Testament, we can ignore the chapters and the verses if they occur only in the margin.

CHAPTER XIV

THE TEXT OF MATTHEW 1:16

There is a curious situation about the text of Matthew 1:16. The Greek manuscripts with the exception of the Ferrar group of minuscules give it as we have it in the Textus Receptus and in Westcott and Hort (both Authorized and Revised Versions): Ἰακὼβ δὲ ἐγέννησεν Ἰωσὴφ τὸν ἄνδρα Μαρίας, ἐξ ἧς ἐγεννήθη Ἰησοῦς ὁ λεγόμενος Χριστός. All the Greek uncials so have it. And yet Plummer in his *Commentary on the Gospel according to St. Matthew* (p. 3) says: "The reading in verse 16 is very uncertain, and it is possible that no Greek MS. has preserved the original text." Sanday in his article *Jesus Christ* in the Hastings *Dictionary of the Bible* (published also as *Outlines of the Life of Christ*) says about the conflicting theories of the text: "We can only note the possibilities; the data do not allow us to decide absolutely between them." And yet Hort takes no notice of it in his "Notes on Select Readings" in Vol. II of *The New Testament in Greek*. Tischendorf devotes less than two lines to a variation in some Old Latin manuscripts (a g′ k q) which have *cui desponsata virgo Maria genuit*, and Tischendorf adds "similiter b c d syr^cu arm al Gaud Op." And q omits *virgo*. One would hardly think that here lies concealed one of the most difficult problems in the textual criticism of the Gospels.

Von Soden boldly prints Ἰακὼβ δὲ ἐγέννησεν τὸν Ἰωσήφ, Ἰωσὴφ δέ ᾧ ἐμνηστεύθη παρθένος Μαριάμ, ἐγέννησεν Ἰησοῦν. Moffatt in his *New Translation of the New Testament* renders thus: "Jacob the father of Joseph, and Joseph (to whom the Virgin Mary was betrothed) the father of Jesus who is called Christ." But Moffatt (*Introduction to the Literature of the New Testament*, 1911, p. 251) says: "The textual problem of 1:16 is not yet settled." But he holds that "the earliest variants" "show traces, variously phrased, of the virgin birth." Von Soden gives the Greek text represented by the Sinaitic Syriac.

It is not yet possible to settle all the points in dispute concerning this passage. The discovery of the Sinai Palimpsest (Sinaitic Syriac) by Mrs. Lewis and Mrs. Gibson in 1892 (published in 1894) intensified the discussion, for this early manuscript reads: "Jacob begat Joseph; Joseph, to whom was betrothed Mary the Virgin, begat Jesus, who is called the Christ." Note the repetition of Joseph. At once it was said by some that this early Syriac document preserves the original text, older than the Greek documents, that here is a denial of the Virgin Birth of Jesus, and that the story of the Virgin Birth was a later addition not in the original text of Matthew. On the other hand it was noted that the Sinaitic Syriac text still had Matt. 1:18–25 which flatly affirmed the Virgin Birth in the message of the angel to Joseph. Hence, if the scribe meant to deny the Virgin Birth in 1:16, he failed to eliminate it in 1:18–25. Besides, in

1:16, the Sinaitic Syriac has the phrase "the Virgin Mary."

A careful study of the reading in the Sinaitic Syriac has led most scholars to the conclusion reached by Mrs. Lewis (*Light on the Four Gospels from the Sinai Palimpsest*, p. 32) that the word "begat" here has a purely legal sense. "Joseph, from a legal point of view only, was the father of our Lord" (p. 34). Thus does Mrs. Lewis argue to save the Sinaitic Syriac from the charge of heresy or Ebionitic influence. She holds that Joseph married Mary before the birth of Jesus so that our Lord was born in wedlock (p. 37). She notes that in Luke 2:5 the Syriac Versions call Mary Joseph's "espoused wife." Streeter (*The Four Gospels*, p. 567) thinks that the reading of the Sinaitic Syriac here "has small claim to be regarded as the true text." He thinks that the name "Joseph" was repeated by dittography (p. 87). He holds that the Sinaitic Syriac was translated from a Greek manuscript of the θ type.

But the Sinaitic Syriac does not stand alone. The Curetonian Syriac has the following text: "Joseph, him to whom was betrothed Mary the Virgin, she who bare Jesus the Messiah." The Greek text behind the Curetonian Syriac is: Ἰακὼβ δὲ ἐγέννησεν τὸν Ἰωσὴφ ᾧ μνηστευθεῖσα παρθένος Μαριὰμ ἣ ἐγέννησεν Ἰησοῦν Χριστόν. It will be seen at once that this text differs radically from that of the Sinaitic Syriac which repeats Joseph and has behind it a Greek text that makes Joseph the subject of ἐγέννησεν with the usual sense "begat" whereas the Curetonian Syriac represents a Greek text that makes ἐγέννησεν mean "bare," a possible sense of the word. It may well be that the Sinaitic

THE TEXT OF MATTHEW 1:16

Syriac is older than the Curetonian which instead of repeating Joseph makes Mary the subject of the verb with the sense of "bare." This idea preserves the teaching about the Virgin Birth in clear form, though both Curetonian and Sinaitic have "Virgin Mary" and the message to Joseph in 1:18–25.

But it is fairly open to question whether the text of the Curetonian Syriac is not independent of the Sinaitic since there are so many variations on this verse. The repetition of Joseph in the Sinaitic may be due to a sense of regularity since the preceding clauses run in that fashion. The scribe may have used "begat" in the purely legal sense. Allen (*Int. Crit. Comm.*, p. 8) thinks that it is probable that the Greek text behind both the Sinaitic and the Curetonian was without the relative clause, "to whom was betrothed Mary the Virgin," which was added in both to make plain that ἐγέννησεν was used in the legal sense. Then the Curetonian Syriac makes Mary the subject instead of Joseph as in the Sinaitic. But it is quite possible that the Sinaitic and the Curetonian worked on a Greek text here independently of each other, though the Curetonian Syriac as a whole is usually considered dependent on the Sinaitic. Allen (p. 8) thinks it possible that the Sinaitic Syriac here represents "a Greek text found nowhere else." He thinks that it is probably nearer the original Greek text than any other now known. That may or may not be true. At any rate it is clear that nothing conclusive against the Virgin Birth can be obtained from the Sinaitic Syriac as many at first supposed. "The verse has been so much and so variously modified, both in the Curetonian

MS. and in the Greek ones, that the shock of surprise which was felt both in the Unitarian camp and in the Orthodox one, at once gave rise to a charge of heresy. This charge, happily, could not be substantiated, for after the publication of the full text it was seen that not only is verse 16 self-contradictory, but the story of the Annunciation, which begins in verse 21, is substantially the same as it is in all Greek MSS." (Mrs. Lewis, *Light on the Four Gospels*, p. 32).

But Burkitt (*Evangelion da-Mepharreshe*, p. 263) thinks that the Sinaitic Syriac is really kin to the Greek text of the Ferrar Group. "The reading of S itself I have come to regard as nothing more than a paraphrase of the reading of the Ferrar Group." What is the reading of the Ferrar Group of Greek minuscules? It is as follows: Ἰακὼβ δὲ ἐγέννησε τὸν Ἰωσὴφ ᾧ μνηστευθεῖσα παρθένος Μαριὰμ ἐγέννησεν Ἰησοῦν τὸν λεγόμενον Χριστόν. The Koridethi Manuscript (θ) has this reading also. It will be seen at once that this is a Greek text very much like the one that was used by the Curetonian Syriac. It appears also in the Armenian Version. The theory about the Ferrar Group of minuscules (346, 543, 826, 828) is that they represent an early uncial. The agreement of the Curetonian Syriac at this point harmonizes with that idea.

Some of the Old Latin Manuscripts preserve a kindred reading. Thus a, g, q, have a reading like that of the Ferrar Group: *Cui desponsata virgo* (q omits *virgo*) *Maria genuit, Jesum qui dicitur* (*vocatur*, g, q) *Christus*. But d k, like the Curetonian Syriac, omit *qui dicitur* thus: *Cui desponsat virgo Maria genuit* (*perperit* d) *Iesum Christum*. The text of the great uncials and of the mass of the minuscules is that which is behind the Authorized Version and the Revised Version. It is as follows: Ἰακὼβ δὲ ἐγέννησεν τὸν Ἰωσὴφ [τὸν ἄνδρα Μαρίας, ἐξ ἧς ἐγεννήθη Ἰησοῦς ὁ λεγόμενος Χριστός. Ordinarily the testimony of all the Greek Manuscripts, uncials and minuscules (save the Ferrar Group) would settle the question. And, as we have seen, it did settle it with Westcott and Hort, who take no notice of variant readings here. But modern scholars have not shared the indifference of Westcott and Hort. Sanday, Zahn, Von Soden, Moffatt, Allen, Burkitt, all show great perplexity about what was the original reading in Matthew 1:16. Zahn is confident (*Evangelium des Matthäus*, p. 66) that the text of the Sinaitic Syriac cannot be the original text because it stands in opposition to Matthew 1:18–25. Allen feels (*Comm.*, p. 8) that it stands nearer to the original Greek than any other. McNeile (*Comm. on Matt.*, p. 4) thinks that "an early alteration was made in the text from which sprang a variety of readings." Evidently so, but which was the original text?

If the Sinaitic Syriac and the Curetonian Syriac agreed instead of disagreeing, we should have a clearer case. And then if the Old Latin a g q and d k agreed instead of disagreeing, it would be simpler. If, once again, the Old Syriac and the Old Latin combined against the old Greek manuscripts, it would look like a Western reading that would challenge credence.

If doctrinal bias be dismissed, for all the readings really preserve the Virgin Birth, we may think of accidental errors due to careless scribes. "That orthodox persons could make slips is shown by (*e*) and also by the Arabic Diat. (Vat. MS., Ciasca's A), ' . . . Joseph, who from her begat Jesus the Messiah.' Burkitt shows it to be probable that 'who from her begat' is a blundering translation of the Pesh. 'from whom was born'" (McNeile, *Matthew*, p. 5). Another instance appears in the Palestinian Syriac Lectionary which has "Joseph the husband of Mary, him from whom was born Jesus." The passive Greek form ἐγεννήθη is here behind this translation, but the scribe has stupidly inserted "him" after "Mary" and has made nonsense of it in so doing.

It is possible that phrases were added without doctrinal purpose or dropped from other motives. The *Dialogue of Timothy and Aquila* has the text of the Greek manuscripts and adds the reading of the Sinaitic Syriac "and Joseph begat Jesus who is called Christ." F. C. Conybeare argued for this conflate reading as the original, but he has won no support. Burkitt thinks that the addition from the Sinaitic Syriac is simply the inference of the Jew in the *Dialogue* and not the statement after quoting the genealogy.

As a matter of fact we run upon snags whatever text we consider to be the original. The change from ἐγεννήθη to ἐγέννησεν is not easy to explain on the assumption that the accepted text is correct. It may have been due to a casual desire to make the whole genealogy alike without thinking of the Virgin Birth controversy. It may after all be the work of an Ebionite who did not carry out his idea consistently.

Vincent Taylor (*The Virgin Birth*, p. 110) says: "We have frankly to admit that no extant reading, as a whole, commends itself as the original text of Matthew 1:16." He adds: "It may be, that is to say, that the text of Matthew 1:16 has found its grave in the readings that we possess." But Mr. Taylor is certain that all the readings preserve the idea of the Virgin Birth: "The original text of Matthew 1:16 implied the Virgin Birth, but it was stated from the unique point of view reflected in the Genealogy itself" (p. 114).

We have to rest content with this conclusion for the present. I confess that I am too much under the influence of Westcott and Hort to agree to any one of the variant readings with such slight support against the solid body of the Greek uncials. I am not ready to say that the Greek uncials are always right. In a few instances all known manuscripts have gone astray. It is abstractly possible that a single Greek manuscript may preserve the true text against all the rest. An old version may be right against the Greek manuscripts. But, when it comes to one manuscript of an old version, the ice gets a bit thin. And yet Souter says that if the Syriac Sinaitic and k of the Old Latin agree against the Greek manuscripts, he is prepared to follow the Syriac Sinaitic and k of the Old Latin rather than Aleph and B (*Mansfield College Essays*, p. 363). But they do not agree here, nor do the Curetonian Syriac and k quite agree in Matthew 1:16.

Sanday dares to suggest a hypothetical original as follows: "If we suppose that the original text ran, Ἰωσὴφ τὸν ἄνδρα Μαρίας ᾗ ἐγέννησεν Ἰησοῦν τὸν λεγόμενον Χριστόν, that would perhaps account for the two divergent lines of variants better than any other. A reading like this appears to be behind the Coptic (Bohairic) Version." Here we have the usual candor and caution of Sanday. But he keeps well within the facts. The variations in the readings are so early and so far apart and so unlike that it is exceedingly difficult to relate them to each other with any degree of satisfaction. It may well be that there is no real connection in all cases. There may be additions here and omissions there. Burkitt thinks that the Syriac Sinaitic is a paraphrase of the reading of the Ferrar Group and that the Curetonian Syriac is a variant from the Sinaitic Syriac (*Evangelion da Mepharreshe*, 2: 262 f.). Perhaps so. But it is difficult for one to strike a note of confidence when the manuscript evidence is so varied and so conflicting.

Moffatt (*Introduction to the Literature of the New Testament*, p. 251) says of Matthew 1: 16: "No hypothesis of literary criticism or textual emendations can disentangle the conception of a virgin-birth from a story which is wrought together and woven on one loom." It is worth something at any rate to come to this clear place. We are not dealing in Matthew 1: 16 primarily with the arguments for and against the Virgin Birth of Jesus. All the documents, including the Sinaitic Syriac, present that idea. It is, then, purely a problem in textual criticism and it should be handled from that standpoint alone.

But it may be confessed frankly that it is a difficult nut to crack as the evidence stands now. One is not able here to employ the usual lines of external evidence. One cannot pit the Neutral against the Western Class.

It is not Pre-Syrian versus Syrian. It is not an Alexandrian scholarly correction. One is not sure that the Sinaitic Syriac reading is Western at all or, if so, it is only in a local sense. Transcriptional evidence is not conclusive. The many variations allow so many suggestions that one becomes confused. Intrinsic evidence fails us also in any final appeal. The weight of the external evidence is for the accepted text. In a way the very number of variations argues against each of them which has such meager support. For the present each scholar will make out his own scheme of the relations of these readings to one another and will have his own theory of the original text.

Something ought to be said about the question of the genealogy in Matthew 1:1–17. The point is whether the author of the Gospel of Matthew copied a document (a family tree) or composed the genealogy from data obtained in several details. If there was an entry in the family record of Joseph, he could, of course, be put down as the father of Jesus. He assumed that position when he married Mary. It is hardly likely that any such record would contain the statement of the Virgin Birth as we have it in Matthew 1:16. But, if the author had such a document, it remains an open question whether he would copy it as it stood, if it had Ἰωσὴφ ἐγέννησεν τὸν Ἰησοῦν. But, if he did that, would he add, as the Sinaitic Syriac has it, "to whom the Virgin Mary was betrothed"? If he added that, he could as well have put it as we have it. So here again we reach no final conclusion.

We seem to be driven into a textual *cul de sac*. If we follow Aleph and B and the rest of the Greek manuscripts save the Ferrar Group, we are open to the charge of traditionalism and of preferring a consistent text that raises no question about the Virgin Birth. The harder text is often the right text. The shorter text is often the true text. This line of argument along the lines of transcriptional evidence goes against the text of Aleph and B. If we seek the text that will best explain the origin of all the rest, the best canon of all in textual criticism, we are confronted by a maze of possibilities. We can start with the text of the Sinaitic Syriac, the shortest and simplest of all, and build a line of possible accretions to it up to the text of Aleph and B and even to that of the *Dialogue of Timothy* and Aquila, but we reach only possibilities, not certainties, at every step. At each turn we face several possibilities. And the text of the Sinaitic Syriac itself is self-contradictory. It has too little and too much. Kenyon (*Textual Criticism of the New Testament*, p. 154) concludes about the text of the Sinaitic Syriac: "The difference of the reading from that of all other authorities makes it highly improbable that it is the true form of the text."

It is a rather lame conclusion to which to come, but it is best to be cautious and right than rash and wrong. We can only go as far as the evidence allows us. All the manuscripts of Matthew 1:16 in all the languages (Greek, Syriac, Old Latin, Egyptian) have the story of the Virgin Birth. Some have it in a shorter form, some in a longer form. All the manuscripts have it clearly in Matthew 1:18–25. In reality all have it in Matthew 1:16 whether we read ἐγεννήθη as most or ἐγέννησεν of Mary in the sense of "bare" or ἐγέννησεν

THE TEXT OF MATTHEW 1:16

of Joseph in the sense of "begat" (legal sense, not physical sense).

We may never be able to disentangle all the variations now known in the manuscripts. On the other hand a single new discovery may set the whole matter clear. Here is a case where the scholar is called upon to be patient and to reserve final judgment till he can get further light. It is much easier to be decisive than to be true, and loyalty to truth is the ear mark of the real scholar. One is beset with the fear, as one closes this discussion, that some of the early copyists and translators were careless or hasty so that we may never get the original text of Matthew 1:16. The only certain result is that, as has been already stated several times, all the readings known to us bear witness to the Virgin Birth of Jesus both in Matthew 1:16 and 1:18–25.

CHAPTER XV

THE MEANING OF JOHN 1:13

A good deal of interest has been aroused as to the true text and the meaning of John 1:13, "which were born, not of blood, nor of the flesh, nor of the will of man, but of God." All the Greek manuscripts read οἵ . . . ἐγεννήθησαν. This reading makes the clause a further description of those who have become sons of God and explains how they are spiritually born, by the new birth or regeneration (verse 12). That is an intelligible idea and probably no modern scholars would question the reading but for one or two things.

One item is that the early fathers who quote John 1:13 give it in the singular ὃς ἐγεννήθη, or *qui natus est*, and make it refer to the birth of Jesus. This is true of Irenæus and Tertullian, and apparently Justin Martyr and Augustine had the singular, not the plural. Irenæus applies the passage directly to Christ: "Not by the will of the flesh, nor by the will of man, but by the will of God, was the Word made flesh" (*Adv. Haer.* 3:16). He thus connects verse 13 with 14, not with 12. Tertullian accuses the Valentinians of changing the singular relative pronoun ὅς to the plural οἵ and the singular verb ἐγεννήθη to the plural ἐγεννήθησαν (*De Carne Christi* xx). In Chapter XXIV he uses the singular against the Ebionites who denied the Virgin

Birth. It must be said that the earliest quotations of this verse give the singular, and this date is a hundred and fifty years earlier than *Codex Vaticanus* and *Codex Sinaiticus*, the two oldest Greek uncials.

The singular appears in two early versions also. The Old Latin *Codex Veronensis* (b) likewise has *qui natus est*. The Curetonian Syriac has the plural "who" but the singular "was born." Burkitt thinks that the singular verb here is a mistake or slip, but Mrs. Lewis argues that it is quite possible that the Sinaitic Syriac had both singular pronoun and singular verb as Augustine quoted, *qui natus est* (*Light on the Four Gospels from the Sinai Palimpsest*, p. 133 f.): "No one can now confidently affirm that the Fourth Gospel contains no allusion to the Virgin Birth." That opinion of the great Syriac scholar and discoverer of the Sinaitic Syriac manuscript of the Gospels is at least enough to make one pause before he brushes aside the evidence for the singular in John 1:13. It should be added that the Sinaitic Syriac is defective in John 1:1-24.

If the Old Syriac and one of the Old Latin documents and the early fathers support the singular, we at least have a very early Western reading. Hort considered it important enough to give a special note in which he calls it "Western." But we have learned that a reading is not necessarily wrong because it is Western. Some of the early Western readings are correct.

It is at least remarkable that such liberals as Harnack and Loisy should argue for the singular in John 1:13, and the undoubted reference to the Virgin Birth of Jesus which, of course, they do not themselves believe. But they hold that the author of the Fourth Gospel did, unless the verse with the singular was added and then changed to the plural. Frederick Blass argued for the singular in John 1:13, as does Zahn quite at length in his *Introduction to the New Testament* (Vol. III, pp. 266, 288, 310). A. E. Brooke, in Peake's *Commentary on the Bible*, also argues for the singular: "The singular leads up well to 14, and the connection with what precedes is good; the sonship of Christians rests on His sonship. In particular the very emphatic threefold negative statement of 13 seems to be directed against some who affirmed the contrary, and such a denial was far more likely to be of Christ's supernatural conception than of the divine begetting of Christians in the spiritual sense."

At any rate we are confronted with an early controversy over the meaning of John 1:13. Some of the early writers accused the Gnostics and Ebionites of tampering with the text and changing the reference from Christ to Christians. Today it is replied that it was the other way, that those who believed in the Virgin Birth of Jesus changed the plural to the singular in order to get a proof text. So there we are. The Greek manuscripts give only the plural, and it will take a good deal of clear proof to get around that fact. Hort argues, however, that there are some sixty-five cases in the New Testament where all the Greek manuscripts are wrong and where we have a primitive error. So we are confronted with the possibility of that being the case in John 1:13.

Once the singular appears in John 1:13 one must admit that it suits the context admirably and leads right up to the statement of the Incarnation in verse 14. There is something, then, to be said for the use of the plural αἱμάτων (bloods) instead of the singular, for according to the Virgin Birth idea Jesus had no human father and there was no union of male and female blood. There is no denying the pertinency of this reading, once it is admitted. But it is too precarious to rest much upon as an argument for the Virgin Birth of Jesus.

It is a much stronger case to see the fact of the Incarnation in verse 14 in connection with the pre-incarnate existence of Christ as the Logos with God in John 1:1. All through the New Testament the Incarnation of Christ is stated and assumed. It is not alone in John's Gospel. It is in Paul's Epistles beyond controversy, as in 2 Corinthians 8:9: "For ye know the grace of our Lord Jesus Christ, that, though he was rich, yet for your sakes he became poor, that ye through his poverty might become rich." Then there is the great Christological passage in Philippians 2:5–11 which sets forth the humiliation and exaltation of Christ in language that not only states the pre-existence of Christ before his birth on earth, but his actual Deity. Then it is not a case of a man who is deified. It is not apotheosis, but the theophany, that we have in Christ. And then Christ is the author of creation and the sustainer of the universe in Colossians 1:15–17. This activity he carried on before the Incarnation.

So then, both in John and in Paul, the main problem is the Incarnation of Christ the Son of God. The Virgin Birth is a detail of the Incarnation. The real battle is over the Incarnation. Paul and John do not mean that God entered by spiritual impression into the heart and life of Jesus so that he became a God-filled man and was lifted into fellowship and communion with God. The rather they both give us the picture of One who was already in existence before the Incarnation as the Son of God who voluntarily came to earth to do his redemptive work for men. It is plain, without any reference to the Virgin Birth, that Paul and John set before us the conception of one who is more than a man, who lived as God's Son before he became the Son of Man, who remained God's Son while the Son of Man, and who today is both Son of God and Son of Man. He took back to Heaven his humanity as he brought to earth his Deity. He was both God and man on earth as he is now in Heaven Jesus Christ, Son of God and Son of man.

Now this picture of Jesus by Paul and John is precisely the one that we have in our oldest known document about Christ, the Logia or Q, as I have shown in *The Christ of the Logia*. That same picture of a supernatural character is seen in Mark's Gospel, in Matthew, and in Luke. The New Testament will be left a torso if the statements about the Deity and the Incarnation of Jesus Christ are all taken out.

There is no getting rid of the Incarnation without also getting rid of Christianity. Now Incarnation is absolutely supernatural. There is no possible way to explain it by any sort of ratiocination. If one is willing to admit and to believe in the fact of the Incarnation, he has no logical ground to stand on in any objection to the fact of the Virgin Birth. There is absolutely nothing anywhere in the New Testament that contradicts the Virgin Birth. It is easy to see why the subject was not a matter of public discussion. The absence of any reference to it in Mark's Gospel means absolutely nothing, for Mark does not even mention the birth of Jesus at all. Surely Mark was not denying his birth. The presence of two clear witnesses for the Virgin Birth of Jesus is really remarkable when all things are considered. In the nature of the case the fact would be known only to a few, but these few would take some pains to make it known ultimately. The account in Matthew is from the standpoint of Joseph, while that in Luke is from the standpoint of Mary. They do not contradict each other. Their very independence strengthens the force of the evidence. I have always felt that the scientific knowledge of Luke and his care as an investigator and writer add great weight to his witness to the fact of the Virgin Birth of Jesus. (See my *Luke the Historian in the Light of Research*.) He took hold of the story from Mary and credited it. That is a significant fact.

Now, one may deny the Incarnation and also dismiss the Virgin Birth with a wave of the hand and retain a sort of intellectual consistency. But, if one accepts the fact of the Incarnation with all of its inevitable implications, I do not see how he can deny the Virgin Birth on the ground of its being a supernatural birth. The Incarnation is supernatural and wholly incomprehensible to us on natural lines. If one does not believe in the Incarnation, it is probably useless to talk with him about the Virgin Birth. But it will be profitable for one who accepts the Incarnation of Christ as a fact, to visualize to himself any process by which the Son of

God who already existed in Heaven came to earth. He will, I believe, have very great difficulty in formulating any theory that is more credible than the Virgin Birth narratives of Matthew and Luke. This line of argument alone does not, of course, prove that the Virgin Birth is a fact. It simply serves as an answer to one who is incredulous, though holding to the Incarnation. One can, of course, leave the whole matter of the Incarnation up in the clouds and not try to offer himself an intellectual substitute for the Virgin Birth. But I agree with the argument of Dr. Briggs, that on philosophical grounds the Virgin Birth is the only intelligible conception of a real Incarnation that has ever been offered. God can and does enter the heart of an individual man, but that is not Incarnation or anything like it.

But let us come back to John 1:13. With the light before us we cannot insist that the singular is clearly, or even probably, the correct text. It is possibly correct. That is all that one can say. But, even so, it is still quite possible that John has the Virgin Birth of Jesus in mind and makes a veiled reference to it. The use of the plural gives a spiritual turn to the language about the physical birth. The three denials with the plural use the language of the physical birth and give that language a metaphorical turn. Very well. After speaking in verse 13 about the spiritual birth of believers as being ἐκ θεοῦ and not of man, the writer adds: "And the Logos became flesh and tabernacled among us." Now in 1:1 the Logos is said to exist in the beginning and to have fellowship with God and to be really God (God's Son, he evidently means).

Now then, the author pointedly asserts that the preexistent Logos σὰρξ ἐγένετο. Note ἐγένετο, not ἦν as in verse 1. Something happened to one already existing. John comes right up to the point of giving us the Virgin Birth. Is his language inconsistent with it? Absolutely not. It is in perfect harmony with it. In fact, one will have difficulty in giving full force to the language of verse 14 without the idea of the Virgin Birth. If Jesus already existed with the Father as in 1:1, how could he become (ἐγένετο) a man already begotten in the ordinary fashion, who was a complete personality? John's language, "became flesh," means clearly that somehow this Logos, who was God, was united with human nature. The Virgin Birth is supernatural, but it at least gives one an intelligent concept, the union in the birth of Jesus of the Spirit of God with Mary. It seems to me that this phrase "became flesh" is John's way of referring to the Virgin Birth narratives in Matthew and in Luke.

It is one of the commonplaces of modern criticism that the Fourth Gospel was later than, and added to the Synoptic Gospels. To be sure, Burney in his *Aramaic Origin of the Fourth Gospel* has raised the question of the early date of the Fourth Gospel. But that view is not yet a working hypothesis. We have to assume that the writer of the Fourth Gospel was familiar with the Virgin Birth narratives in Matthew and Luke. Very well, then. Does he mean to endorse them or to correct them? He most certainly does not correct or deny them. I think that John endorses them in his own metaphysical way. His very language "became flesh" means incarnation. That is not the language employed about an ordinary birth. We do not speak of children becoming flesh. John's language about the Logos points directly back to 1:1.

Nor is this all. In 1:18 the two oldest manuscripts, *Codex Vaticanus* and *Codex Sinaiticus*, give us the text of Westcott and Hort, μονογενὴς θεός, "only begotten God," not "only begotten Son." This is the true text, and this phrase combines verses 1 and 14. Then in 1:18 we have the express combination of Deity and humanity in Jesus Christ. He is still God while man. He is not man become God, as so many modern theologians want us to believe. He is God become man. This is the heart of Christianity, the Incarnation of God's Son.

But it is worth while to look at the rest of the Fourth Gospel to see if we can detect any allusion to the Virgin Birth or to the slander that the Jews started about the birth of Jesus, that he was a bastard, the son of a man named Panthera. In 1:45 Philip describes Jesus to Nathanael as the son of Joseph of Nazareth. Certainly Philip would know nothing of the Virgin Birth of Jesus, and assuredly Jesus passed among men as the son of Joseph. So then this passage has no real bearing on the Virgin Birth. In 1:49 Nathanael does not hesitate to call Jesus the Son of God, as the Baptist had testified in 1:34. In 3:18 we have the expression, "the only begotten Son of God," which at least means that Jesus is the Son of God in a sense not true of other men. This charge the Jews made against Jesus in 5:18, "but he also called God his own Father, making himself equal with God." This charge Jesus not only did not deny, but proceeded to prove by pungent and powerful arguments, which I have presented in *The Divinity of Christ in the Gospel of John*.

The line of argument in John 5 does not prove the Virgin Birth, but it shows that the Father and the Son hold a relation in nature and in work not at all true of others. But in Chapter VI Jesus expressly asserted to the Galilean crowd in the synagogue in Capernaum that he was the bread of life come down from Heaven (6: 35, 38, 41). This daring claim was understood to mean that he was not like ordinary men, for the Jews took it up and murmured at him because he said: "I am the bread that came down out of Heaven." They retorted: "Is not this fellow the son of Joseph, whose father and mother we know? How does he now say, I have come down from Heaven?" They clearly understood Jesus to make a claim to a different origin from that accepted by them, that he was the son of Joseph and Mary. This claim raises the question whether Jesus himself did not know that Joseph was not his actual father. The knowledge that he was in reality the Son of God alone explains the claims that Jesus makes both in the Synoptic Gospels and in the Fourth Gospel.

In John 8: 19 the Pharisees make a sharp retort that may refer to slanderous reports about the birth of Jesus: "Where is your Father?" And still plainer is the fling made by the Pharisees in 8: 41: "We were not born of fornication," as if they thought he was. In a moment of heat such a bitter word was hurled at Jesus. He passes it by, of course, and proceeds to show that they are in reality not the children of Abraham except by birth, but have become children of the devil by character (8:44). It is not hard to see that this was an occasion of great tension, and one can almost see the flaming fires in the volcano of passion.

It should never be forgotten that Jesus accepted the words of Thomas and praised him for saying them: "My Lord and my God" (John 20:28). He knew God as his Father. But Jesus did not disown Mary, as his mother. He thought of her tenderly as he died upon the cross and provided for her welfare (John 19:25-27). There is no record of any special interest of Jesus in Joseph except that he was a dutiful and obedient boy (Luke 2:51). It is probable that Joseph died before Jesus reached maturity. It is likely, as already said, that Mary told Jesus of his real parentage after Joseph's death. At any rate, he has the constant consciousness that he is the Son of God in a sense not true of others. This sense of peculiar relationship with the Father dominates the thoughts and acts of Jesus in a way hardly consonant with a man born of a human father.

So then we conclude that the whole atmosphere of the Fourth Gospel is consonant with the idea of the Virgin Birth as told in Matthew and Luke and as known by John. This idea of the peculiar origin of Jesus pervades the Gospel of John from beginning to end. It makes it practically certain that, when he wrote the words, "The Logos became flesh," he was referring to the Virgin Birth of Jesus who then as the Son of God came into our human nature as the Son of man. That being true, it is not a matter of great importance what the real text of John 1:13 is. If the singular, ὅς ... ἐγεννήθη should ever prove to be genuine, it would be discounted by those who reject the Virgin Birth as of no more value than John 1:1, 14, 18. There the Incarnation stands out clearly.

CHAPTER XVI

THE IMPLICATIONS IN LUKE'S PREFACE

The article of Professor H. J. Cadbury, in the *Expositor* of December, 1922, on "The Knowledge claimed in Luke's Preface" interested me very much. It is certainly wholly to the good to have a fresh and full presentation of the facts concerning the connotations of παρακολουθέω. Such a careful study has been much needed. Dr. Cadbury has done it with more than his usual care, and it supplements well his *Commentary on the Preface of Luke* in part i of Vol. II. of *The Beginnings of Christianity*. There is not much save one point in either the *Commentary* or the *Expositor* article to which one can object. It is nearly all to the good. He rightly shows that παρακολουθέω etymologically and literally means *to follow at one's side*. Some early writers took it in this literal sense and understood πᾶσιν as referring to persons (masculine, not neuter). That in itself is, of course, possible. Only the actual context can determine whether the literal or the figurative meaning of a verb is meant by the writer.

In the figurative sense, which is rightly found here by Dr. Cadbury, he suggests three possible uses and gives examples of each. One is following what is read as in a preface (by the reader, not the writer). A second is keeping in touch with things done, with a

THE IMPLICATIONS IN LUKE'S PREFACE 187

course of events. Dr. Cadbury adds: "This broad meaning is probably to be accepted here." He further says: "It may include reliance upon written information, as is well shown by cases where a letter is said to be written in order that the recipient may keep in touch with events." The third use is "actual presence or participation in the events." On this point Dr. Cadbury makes a real contribution of freshness and force. If the word is capable of this sense, then the author of the Gospel of Luke and of the Acts claims to be in part at least a participant in, or contemporary of, the events. We know that this is true of the second part of Acts (the "we" sections), and there is no reason, so far as we know, why it may not be true of the life of Jesus, unless Luke (or the author) was born near the middle of the first century instead of near the beginning of it.

Dr. Cadbury rightly sees that, if there is truth in this meaning, then the author wrote both books fairly early and had himself personal knowledge of some (or many) of the things of which he writes. Dr. Cadbury thinks this "new consideration" the most convincing argument for the Lucan authorship, which has not hitherto impressed him very greatly.

But it is the denial by Dr. Cadbury of any research on the part of Luke that calls for protest on my part. "There appears to be no warrant for assigning to the word the sense of deliberate investigation, although Luke's apologists love thus to modernize it. The writer's information had (notice the perfect tense) come to him as the events took place; it was not the result of special reading and study. His acquaintance with the subject, whatever its degree of intimacy, was something already in his possession. The perfect tense is often thus used of this verb and this is its meaning."

It is this paragraph that challenges one's scepticism on several important points. One is Dr. Cadbury's interpretation of the perfect active participle παρηκολουθηκότι. The perfect tense here does mean that, "his acquaintance with the subject, whatever its degree of intimacy, was something already in his possession" *before he began to write the book*. It does not mean that "the writer's information had (notice the perfect tense) come to him as the events took place." The very structure of the sentence places παρηκολουθηκότι (whatever it means) as a state of completion be ore γράψαι. It is wholly gratuitous, and I think misleading, to say that the perfect tense conveys here the idea that Luke's information came to him "as the events took place." That special idea is not what the perfect active participle means. It means simply that the process involved (παρηκολουθηκότι) was at an end before Luke proceeded to write (γράψαι). There is absolutely nothing in the perfect tense itself to suggest any notion of "as the events took place." The perfect tense with some verbs may have the resultant sense of "broken continuity," "a series of links rather than a line" (Robertson, *Grammar of the Greek New Testament in the Light of Historical Research*, p. 896; Moulton, *Prolegomena*, p. 144.) But this idea is due to the special meaning of the verb, not to the meaning of the perfect tense. The meaning of the verb affects the perfect tense in such instances. But one cannot turn it round and urge

THE IMPLICATIONS IN LUKE'S PREFACE 189

that the perfect tense calls for such a meaning in the verb. The special use of παρακολουθέω may or may not suggest the idea of broken continuity, but that idea does not come out of the perfect tense. Luke does mean to say with all positiveness that he was prepared to write before he began to write.

Dr. Cadbury puts, I think, too narrow a meaning on the words "investigation" and "research." He denies "deliberate investigation" on Luke's part. "It was not the result of special reading or study." Now, I submit that there is nothing in the meaning of παρακολουθέω (whatever meaning one accepts) or in the context of Luke's Preface to justify these words. It is putting the negative side beyond the warrant of the known facts. It is not clear precisely what Dr. Cadbury means by "research." His last words in the *Expositor* (p. 420) are: "At any rate he says nothing of research." In the *Commentary* (p. 501) he says: "It may include reliance upon written information." If the sense of reading be involved, Dr. Cadbury says: "If this interpretation is adopted here, Luke is claiming to have read the διηγήσεις which the preceding writers had composed." He certainly makes that claim. He introduces the Preface with ἐπειδήπερ which gives the reason that prompted him to write (ἔδειξε κἀμοὶ γράψαι). I see no escape from this interpretation of Luke's sentence. He does not say that he incidentally glanced at a few feeble attempts in writing; but relied chiefly on his own personal knowledge obtained otherwise. He says that he was stirred to his task of writing by what others had written (see my *Luke the Historian in the Light of Research*,

p. 44) by these previous efforts. We know that he made constant use of two of them (the *Logia* or Q and *Mark's Gospel*). If this is not "research," "deliberate investigation," "special reading and study," one is at a loss to know what it is. Every one is entitled to his own opinion, of course, but it seems to me that Luke's known and verifiable use of Q and Mark, forbids our saying that "he says nothing of research." To me the natural inference is quite the other way. His careful use of Q and Mark argues that he made like use of the other written sources known to him.

It is not necessary to know precisely what particular shading of meaning we are to give to παρακολουθεῖν in Luke's Preface. In point of fact Dr. Cadbury is by no means clear in his own views on that point. "Perhaps personal presence is more than the verb παρηκολουθηκότι actually claims. Possibly it was just the kind of verb that included both presence and indirect though contemporary information, and could be used by one who wished to suggest the utmost knowledge without defining too specifically how intimate that knowledge was." I see nothing in this statement that goes too far except the use of "indirect." Dr. Cadbury here admits that Luke may wish "to suggest the utmost knowledge without defining how intimate that knowledge was." Well, then, why insist on the adjective "indirect"? Some of it may have been "indirect," but certainly the use of Q and Mark was not "indirect." There is nothing in the word παρηκολουθηκότι or the context inconsistent with the use of "direct" information also.

THE IMPLICATIONS IN LUKE'S PREFACE

I sincerely concur in the conclusion of Dr. Cadbury that "the possibility must be left open that the author is claiming in the very beginning of his work to have been long in such close contact with the series of events which he unfolds as to be possessed of first-hand contemporary knowledge about them, and that perhaps he means to claim the knowledge of an actual eyewitness." I am bound to demur to the closing sentence: "At any rate he says nothing of research," as if that failure proves that "it was not the result of special reading and study." Nothing that Dr. Cadbury has produced warrants so positive a denial. Dr. Cadbury admits that "the verb is used in so many senses that absolute certainty is impossible." And yet he pointedly denies one of the possible uses of the verb.

Dr. Cadbury draws a distinction between careful reading and philosophic reflexion and research that is not clear to me. "At most it would mean only the intelligent and attentive understanding of what is read or told, not deliberate inquiry." We know the use that Luke made of Q and Mark. Was that "deliberate research" or merely "the intelligent and attentive understanding of what is read"? And what is the difference? Is one to say that Luke merely copied Q and Mark without reflexion? The facts in Luke's Gospel refute that idea.

Dr. Cadbury makes the point that when παρακολουθέω occurs in Hellenistic writers "it invariably applies not to the writer but to the reader." If Luke employs the word in that sense in his Preface, he likewise refers to the works of others that he has read, not to his own work. He would have in mind διηγήσεις of previous writers which he had read, as Dr. Cadbury properly observes.

It will be seen that at almost every point I find myself in agreement with Dr. Cadbury's fresh and illuminating discussions of Luke's Preface save in his denial of research by the author. It is quite likely that some writers have insisted too strongly that παρακολουθεῖν can mean nothing else but to make research. Dr. Cadbury has done a good service in showing the variety of uses of this interesting verb. But he has, I think, gone too far in urging that the author's information "was not the result of special reading and study." Dr. Cadbury offers no real proof for that denial. The very context in Luke's Preface disproves it.

The use of ἄνωθεν with παρηκολουθηκότι falls in also with the idea of careful preparation before writing.

www.ingramcontent.com/pod-product-compliance
Lightning Source LLC
Chambersburg PA
CBHW071423160426
43195CB00013B/1783